dorp and St Francis Bay in the Diocese of Port Elizabeth, where he had been Parish Council chairman, as well as Parish Secretary. Both he and his wife Sylvia are Extraordinary Ministers of the Eucharist - Frank celebrated his 30th anniversary as a Eucharistic Minister in October 2020 - and Frank is also a Proclaimer and Liturgical Leader, conducting Communion Services for his community in the absence of a priest.

He and Sylvia have one son, Ryan, who lives in New Zealand with his wife Elaine, and two little boys, Liam and Torben.

Frank and Sylvia are now resident in New Zealand with their family. The live on a farm north of Auckland, not far from the towns of Silverdale and Orewa, and attend Mass in the historic Puhoi Church of Sts Peter & Paul, where Frank is once more a proclaimer and Minister of the Eucharist.

Dedication

This book is dedicated to the memory of the late Fr Paul Fahy, beloved pastor and mentor, who served the Catholic community of the Eastern Cape for 50 years.

It is further dedicated to the memory of my parents, Denis & Gladys Nunan.

Do You Speak Catholic?

The Little Book of Catholic Words - Definitions, Explanations and Illustrations

Revised Second Edition

Compiled by

Frank Nunan

Foreword by Bishop Vincent Zungu OFM

Who is Frank Nunan?

Frank Nunan is a journalist and editor by profession who received his initial journalistic training in the then Rhodesia on the Bulawayo Chronicle. He has also worked on South African newspapers such as The Star and the Sunday Times, and was active in the marketing and IT fields for many years after leaving journalism.

After moving to the Eastern Cape from Johannesburg in 2011, he launched SA Catholic Online in 2013 as a Catholic internet resource, and simultaneously began his publishing facilitation business, offering proof-reading editing and self-publishing services to Catholic authors. This was expanded to the secular world in 2016 with the launch of Write-On Publishing.

He has to date published more than 150 books, including more than 35 Catholic books or books by Catholic authors.

He has also been active in internet services, and has developed and at one stage hosted about a dozen parish and other Catholic websites, including the Diocese of Port Elizabeth site, and that of Radio Veritas, South Africa's Catholic radio station. His association with Radio Veritas extended to a weekly 10-minute slot in which he mainly discusses the Church's use of the internet and suggests various websites and other online resources for listeners. He has continued this broadcast on a fortnightly basis following his move to New Zealand

He was active in the affairs of his home parish, the Kouga Catholic Community of Jeffreys Bay, Humans-

What they said about "Do You Speak Catholic?"

"This book is a valuable resource for the candidates who are preparing to be received into the Church, for the catechumens, the sponsors and catechists who are involved in RCIA, for the altar servers and lay ministers who assist us to worship, and for postulants, novices and young seminarians."
- Bishop Vincent Zungu OFM.

"I am sold on the book! It is an interesting description of things Catholic. I will think many "ordinary" good Catholics do not know half of what you describe so beautifully in the book. As for my ignorance, I found three things I did not know of or had even heard of until I read your book. So you see, I am sure you will be teaching a few bishops in the process!"
- Bishop Frank Nubuasah SVD.

"A useful lexicon of Catholic lingo"
- Günther Simmermacher, Editor, Southern Cross.

"Every RCIA class in every parish should have at least one."
- Michael Mahony, Lay Theologian and Author.

"Every Parish should have three or four of these books"
- Deacon Walter Middleton.

Published by:

SA Catholic Online Books
In Association with Write-On Publishing
frank@sacatholiconline.org
www.sacatholiconline.org
www.write-on-publishing.com

Edited By Frank Nunan
Cover & Book Design: Frank Nunan

Imprimatur & Nihil Obstat:

His Excellency Bishop Vincent Mduduzi Zungu OFM

Diocese of Port Elizabeth.

11 May, 2020

Revised Second Edition - May 2024

ISBN: 978-1-7764848-4-3

For more information please see
www.write-on-publishing.com

Also by this Author:

My First Book of Catholic Words

The Christmas Story

Both these books are colour-in workbooks for young children.

Preface

What is an aspergillum? What is the difference between a thurible and a thurifer? What is the difference between a homily and a sermon?

Catholicism, like many institutions and organisations, has its own "jargon" and the words that are used in the context of Faith and Worship can be totally mystifying to the uninitiated (and even to the initiated!) Many words used in our Faith have completely different meanings from the same words in the secular world.

How did the idea for this book come into being?

Early in 2019, my wife and I visited New Zealand, where our son and his family live. It was our first visit, and the first time we had actually seen our grandchildren "in the flesh", as it were. While we were there, we attended Sunday Mass at St Mary's Catholic Church in Northcote, North Auckland – a beautiful church and a vibrant community, ably and joyfully shepherded by Fr Lio Pator.

During our stay, the Parish was preparing to celebrate the 50th anniversary of the consecration and dedication of their church. As part of these preparations, Fr Lio gave a couple of presentations which I found fascinating. The first was called "Sacred Spaces" and dealt with the church building and its various parts and functions. Words like "narthex" and "nave", "ambo" and "ambry" were explained and defined. While I knew most of the terms, it was good to hear them used and described in context.

He followed this presentation up with another called "Sacred Vessels, Vestments and Gestures". Again, most of these were familiar but to hear them explained and once more put into context was very enlightening.

I approached Fr Lio and asked him for copies of the presentations, which he very graciously gave me, and I brought them back to South Africa.

A few months later the opportunity arose for me to present them, slightly adapted, to the members of our parish (Kouga Catholic Community of Jeffreys Bay, Humansdorp and St Francis Bay) – to great appreciation and enthusiasm.

I thought nothing more of them, and then one day later that year, while researching for my weekly Radio Veritas spot, I found a document called "Catholic Words", meant for children. It explained, with pictures, a small number of everyday Catholic words. This triggered something in my head, and remembering the response to the presentations, I thought "Why not compile a booklet of Catholic Words and Definitions". Why not indeed, although little did I realise what I was letting myself in for!

The idea is not to get into any depth but merely to try to offer brief and hopefully easily understandable definitions and explanations for "Catholic" words, some of which people hear often and may not be too sure about, others which are more obscure. Yet others have a variety of meanings in different contexts (such as the word "Ordinary").

Why include the obscure and even obsolete words? Well, while they may not be in everyday use, people still come across them and wonder what they mean and where they originate. For example, who wears a biretta these days? Not many priests that I know of - except Fr S'milo Mngadi, one of my authors, and of course "Father Brown" in the popular TV series!

This is not intended to be a liturgical or theological book – I was told in no uncertain terms that I was "not qualified" for that, which is a truth to which I fully subscribe! If I have strayed into the realm of theology or liturgy, it has not been intentional, and I humbly apologise.

As an editor and publisher, I have always been fascinated by words, and whenever I hear a new one, I try to find out what it means. These days that is relatively easy to do – simply type the word into Google, and hey presto, there you have it!

So if it is so easy to look up words, why compile a book?

One of the things I discovered in researching this book is that some of the definitions and explanations you find on Google are long and tedious, and often don't actually come to the point, leaving you more mystified than ever. They are often written in language that is intended for "learned people". The sources sometimes even contradict each other, leaving you unsure of where the truth lies.

The book has the advantage of having all the words in one place, in alphabetical order, making them easy to find. The definitions are generally brief and to the point, without going into protracted theological explanations and history.

Not trusting my own judgement, I submitted the first draft of the manuscript to three separate "authorities" (my word, not theirs), lay theologian and author Mike Mahony, Deacon Philip Teulon of our parish, and former Apostolic Administrator of the Diocese of Port

Elizabeth, Msgr Brendan Deenihan, for their comments and thoughts. All three were enthusiastic about the project, and were extremely helpful, for which I am eternally grateful.

I also acknowledge and thank Fr Lio Pator of the St Mary's Catholic Church in Northcote, Auckland, New Zealand for his original inspiration.

There is one other person without whom none of this would have been possible - my dearest wife Sylvia. I thank her for her unceasing encouragement and above all patience, and for her support and love.

This project grew and grew! I would find myself waking up at three in the morning with yet another word running around in my head! I would look up the definition of one word, and almost invariably, that definition would yield another word or phrase which I had not thought about or had forgotten. The list of words and phrases in this book is not by any means complete, and I am sure just about every reader will say: "Well, what about this one, or that one?" Please send them to me, and I will be sure to include them, if, by the grace of God, there is a second edition of the book.

I am hoping the book finds resonance with ordinary Catholics, and as Mike Mahony put it: "It should be handed out in every RCIA class in every parish." From your lips to the ears of God, Mike!

For the past 12 years, three Catholic institutions played a major role in my life. They have helped shape me into what I have become as a person and a Catholic communicator, and have been supportive and encouraging in all my Catholic endeavours, as well as in my publishing and communications work. These are my own parish, the Kouga Catholic Community and especially our late pastor Fr Paul Fahy, the Diocese of Port Elizabeth and its bishop, Vincent Mduduzi Zungu OFM - not to mention his secretary, Rebecca Huntly - and before him the Apostolic Administrator, Msgr Brendan Deenihan, and finally Radio Veritas and the late Fr Emil Blazer OP.

When I launched my SA Catholic Online website in 2013, Fr Emil and Olinda Orlando of Radio Veritas were on the phone even before the story in *The Southern Cross*, South Africa's then weekly Catholic newspaper, hit the streets. I have been a part of the Radio Veritas family ever since, with a weekly spot called *Frank-ly Catholic*, in which I explore how the Church is using the internet for evangelisation, formation and communication. I have continued these, albeit on a fortnightly basis, since moving to New Zealand in 2023.

This is the second edition of the book, which now contains more than 300 words, phrases and explanations! This edition came about as I began to realise that I had neglected to include a number of words that were in regular use. As I began my research into these additional words, once again, the project snowballed!

I also decided to add a section on Catholic Symbols.

God Bless

Frank Nunan
Revised Second Edition
Auckland - May 2024.

Foreword

By Bishop Vincent Zungu OFM

Diocese of Port Elizabeth

Words, whether they are nouns, verbs, adverbs, adjectives, prepositions or phrases may appear small and insignificant, but they are essential building blocks of language in every culture, society, civilisation, institution and other organisations that are secular, religious or mixed. They are loaded with meaning and have incredible power to inspire, educate, motivate, excite, incite, dissuade, fascinate, stimulate and stretch our imagination.

This, in turn, sets us on a long journey from the mind, to the heart and move us to action which literally puts our hands and feet into motion. "Of all the magic words in existence, words of kindness create the greatest transformation spells" *(Richelle E Goodrich)*.

This inspiring and fascinating book of Catholic Words and Definitions which are used in the context of Faith and Worship is the fruit of prayer, deep reflection, thorough research, study, discernment and actual compilation by a seasoned journalist, a versatile (and all-round) Christian publisher of note and communicator who successfully navigates his way on all networks: online, radio and publications. It is a living testimony of his faith.

When I first read "Do You Speak Catholic? The Little Book of Catholic Words" I was filled with tremendous joy of being a Catholic. I felt privileged to belong to the Church, the living Body of Christ *(1 Cor12:27)* which is also affectionately referred to, understood, known and celebrated as the Family of God here in Africa. I, therefore, invite all the Faithful who would like to familiarise themselves with Catholic language, that is, to say our "Mother-tongue" in the form of these words, expressions, definitions, explanations and illustrations to read this book. I am sure it will help deepen your identity, give you a sense of appreciation of our heritage and enhance your full, conscious, meaningful and active participation in the Eucharist, the source and summit of all our Christian life. It is in the Eucharist that our transforming encounter with Christ takes place, in the most profound way.

This book is a valuable resource for the candidates who are preparing to be received into the Church, for the catechumens, the sponsors and catechists who are involved in the RCIA, for the altar servers, lay ministers — sacristans, proclaimers and communion givers who assist us to worship in truth and in spirit, and for those who are in initial stages of formation and training: postulants, novices and young seminarians.

I also recommend it sincerely to all the People of God who take the mandate of Jesus Christ seriously to "Go, therefore, make disciples of all nations; baptise them in the name of the Father and of the Son and of the

Holy Spirit, and teach them to observe all the commands I gave you"*(Mt 28:19)*.

Indeed, it is a fitting tribute to Fr Paul Fahy, "a shepherd after God's own heart" *(Jer 3:15)*, a priest and a missionary who was always passionate about evangelisation. He worked very hard to bring the Joy of the Gospel to all the people he served in the Diocese of Port Elizabeth over a period of 50 years.

May his ministry continue to bear fruits in abundance and his memory live forever!

Bishop Vincent Mduduzi Zungu OFM

11ᵗʰ May 2020

ORATORY
LECTIONARY
TRIREGNUM
TRANSEPT
SACRAMENTARY
INCARDINATION
CHANCERY
ASPERGILLUM
ORDINARY
MOZZETTA SYNOD BEATIFICATION EPICLESIS KERYGMA
BASILICA DALMATIC SACRAMENTAL
PALLIUM CINCTURE HOMILY CATECHUMEN RELIQUARY
MITRE CATECHETICS FRACTION NUNCIO
HUMERAL CROTALUS CURIA BIRETTA SCAPULAR
DISCERNMENT
ENCYCLICAL
SOLEMNITY
DICASTERY
HOLY RITE
VEIL
CHRISM
BREVIARY
ASPERSORIUM
STIPEND
COLUMBARIUM
PULPIT
ZUCCHETTO
MAGISTERIUM
INDULGENCE
NARTHEX

The A – Z of Catholic Words and Phrases

A

Abstinence

Abstinence is defined as the practice of restraining oneself from indulging in something, typically alcohol or sex. However, in the Catholic context, abstinence is defined explicitly as abstaining from consuming red meat on given days, traditionally on all Fridays of the year. The Law of Abstinence has, to a certain extent, been relaxed in many countries, and now usually only applies to Fridays in Lent. Abstinence is also prescribed in conjunction with fasting on days such as Ash Wednesday and Good Friday.

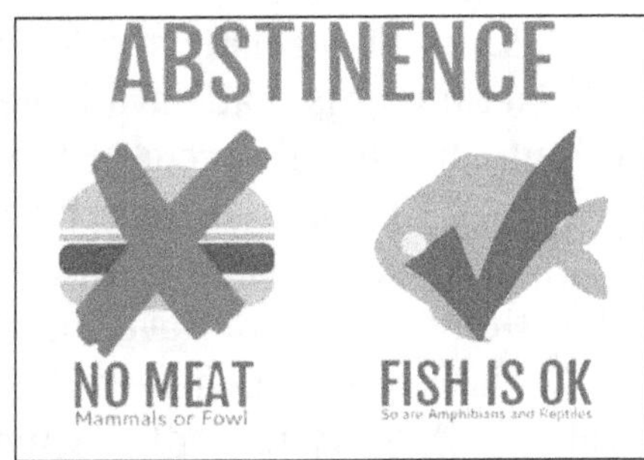

Acolytes/Altar Servers

Previously an acolyte was a cleric promoted to the fourth and highest minor order in the Latin Church, ranking next to a sub-deacon. The primary function of an acolyte was to light the candles on the altar, to carry them in procession and during the solemn singing of the Gospel; to prepare wine and water for the sacrifice of the Mass; to assist the sacred ministers at the Mass and other public services of the Church - all functions now carried out by altar servers. However, in 1973 Pope Paul VI abolished "minor orders" with the apostolic letter *Ministeria Quaedam*, but kept the role of acolyte, calling it instead a "ministry". Currently, the term is more commonly used to refer to altar servers and even more specifically, those who carry the candles at Mass.

Adoration

This is a Eucharistic service in which the Blessed Sacrament is made available to be adored by the faithful. This usually occurs either when the Eucharist is exposed (in a Monstrance, or simply in a ciborium) during a devotion such as Holy Hour or benediction. Adoration is a sign of devotion to and worship of Jesus Christ, who we believe to be present Body, Blood, Soul, and Divinity, under the appearance of the consecrated host. Perpetual Adoration is when the Blessed Sacrament is left exposed constantly.

Advent

Advent is the season observed by the Church (and most Christian denominations) as a time of expectant waiting and preparation for the celebration of the birth of Christ at Christmas. It includes the four Sundays preceding Christmas, and also marks the beginning of the new liturgical year.

Advent Wreath/Candles

An Advent wreath is usually made of holly or evergreen branches that hold three purple candles and a rose one. These candles represent the four Sundays of Advent. One purple candle is lit the first week, two purple candles the second week, two purple and one rose (representing joy) the third week, and, in the last week of Advent, all four are lit.

The light of the candles represents the light of Christ, who will come into the world at Christmas. The circular shape of the wreath stands for eternity because it has no beginning or end. Advent wreaths are usually displayed in the home on a table or stand. Some traditions include a fifth candle (white) in the centre of the wreath, which is lit on Christmas Day to symbolise the Light of Christ.

Alb

The alb is a long white gar-ment which flows from the shoulders to ankles, and has long sleeves extending to the wrist. It is worn by the priest under his chasuble and by the deacon under his dalmatic. The spiritual purpose is to remind the priest of his baptism, when he was clothed in white to signify his freedom from sin, the purity of

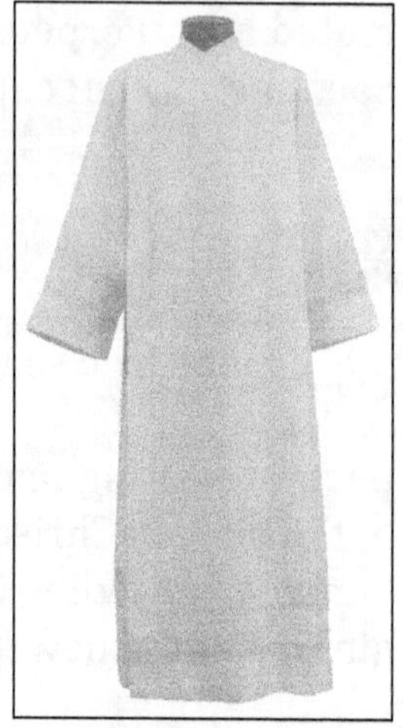

new life, and Christian dignity. The design of the alb is based on typical Greek and Roman clothing worn in the first century. The word *alb* comes from the Latin *albus*, which means white - a colour symbolising purity. For a wonderful explanation of all the vestments worn by the priest during Mass please see this You-Tube video: https://youtu.be/aCccFmnsqyg.

Almsgiving

Almsgiving is the act of donating money or goods to the poor or performing other acts of charity as a form of penance. Charity, or almsgiving, is an outward sign of Christian love for others. Generally, it involves some type of sacrifice on behalf of the giver in order to provide for the needs of the other.

Altar

The altar is the place where the bread and wine are consecrated during Mass. It is also known as the Table of Sacrifice. The altar is also where the Monstrance containing the Blessed Sacrament is placed for Exposition and Adoration. One or more relics of martyrs are commonly set into the altar. In the primitive church and in the catacombs, the altar was usually a slab over the tomb of a martyr. When an altar is dedicated after a new church is built or an old one is remodelled, it is sprinkled with holy water and anointed with Chrism oil before it is "dressed" in a white altar-cloth, much like a person who is baptised.

Altar Candles

There should be at least two lit candles placed on or near the altar at every Mass. These candles are called altar candles.

Altar candles should be made mostly of beeswax, which represents the pure flesh of Christ. The wick represents the soul of Christ, and the flame symbolises his divinity. A Mass can't begin without the altar candles being lit. Candles were initially used for the very practical purpose of illuminating the catacombs where Mass was said, and later to light the church and the sanctuary. They then gained a more profound spiritual symbolism – the Light of Christ and the Light of the Word.

Ambo

An Ambo is a lectern from which the Scripture readings are proclaimed during Mass. These days, in most churches, ambo is also where the priest or deacon delivers the homily or sermon and where the petitions or Prayers of the Faithful are read. The ambo is also known as the Altar or Table of the Word, and is said by some to have equal stature with the Altar or Table of Sacrifice, as together they enable the celebration of the Eucharist as a whole. Non-liturgical announcements, presentations, and so forth should **not** be made from the ambo. While the ambo can be used for homilie, it should not be confused with a pulpit.

Ambry

This is a niche, recess, cupboard or cabinet where the three Holy Oils are kept. It may be placed on or near the Sanctuary.

These oils are used at Baptisms, Confirmation, Priestly Ordination, and to anoint the sick. An ambry often has glass doors and a light inside to display the Holy Oils and to show that they are sacred and important.

Amen

A Hebrew word meaning truly; it is so; let it be done, and signifying agreement with what has been said. The prayers of the New Testament, the Church's liturgy, and the Creeds conclude with amen. Jesus used the word to introduce solemn assertions, to emphasise their trustworthiness and authority.

Amice

The amice is a piece of white linen, rectangle in shape, with two long cloth ribbons. It is placed around the priest's neck, covering the clerical collar, and then tied by crisscrossing the ribbons in the front (to form a St Andrew's cross), bringing them around the back, around the waist and tied in a bow. The practical purpose of the amice was to conceal the normal clerical clothing of the wearer and to absorb any perspiration from the head and neck. This vestment is no longer obligatory in the Catholic Church. It is, however, still worn if the alb does not cover the clothing underneath.

Angelus

The Angelus is a short devotion in honour of the Incarnation, repeated three times each day – morning (6 am), noon, and evening (6 pm) - at the sound of the Angelus bells. It consists mainly of the triple repetition of the "Hail Mary", to which have been added three short introductory verses with responses, and a concluding short verse and prayer. The devotion derives its name from the first word of the three short verses - *Angelus Domini Nuntiavit Mariæ* ("The Angel of the Lord declared unto Mary").

The Angelus

The angel of the Lord declared unto Mary.
R. And she conceived of the Holy Spirit.
(Hail Mary . . .)
Behold the handmaid of the Lord.
R. Be it done unto me according to thy word.
(Hail Mary ...)
And the Word was made flesh.
R. And dwelt among us.
(Hail Mary ...)

Pray for us, O holy Mother of God.
R. That we may be made worthy of
the promises of Christ.

Let us pray: Pour forth, we beseech thee, O Lord, thy grace into our hearts; that, we to whom the incarnation of Christ, thy Son, was made known by the message of an angel, may by his passion and cross, be brought to the glory of his resurrection, through the same Christ our Lord. Amen.

Anointing

Anointing is a symbol of the Holy Spirit's presence in the sacraments of Confirmation, Baptism and Holy Orders. It represents the fulfillment of prophecies in the Old Testament about the anointing of Jesus as the Messiah, which means the "one anointed by the Holy Spirit". Anointing is also part of the liturgical rites of the catechumenate (the period of initiation into the Church).

Anointing of the Sick

In the Catholic Church, the anointing of the sick, previously known as Extreme Unction, is a sacrament administered to a Catholic "who, having reached the age of reason, begins to be in danger due to sickness or old age" (Code

of Canon Law). It is administered by a priest. The sacrament involves prayer and the anointing of the body with the oil of the sick. It is not necessary for the person to actually be on the point of death to receive this sacrament.

Annulment

In the Canon Law of the Church, an annulment is properly called a "Declaration of Nullity", because according to Catholic doctrine, the marriage of baptised persons is a sacrament and, once consummated and thereby confirmed, cannot be dissolved as long as the parties to it are alive. A "Declaration of Nullity" is not dissolution of a marriage, but merely the legal finding that a valid marriage was never contracted. It is the popular word to indicate an official declaration by an ecclesiastical authority that a marriage contract did not exist from the beginning. It is a recognition of the fact that a marriage has never come into being in spite of there having been a proper marriage ceremony.

Apse

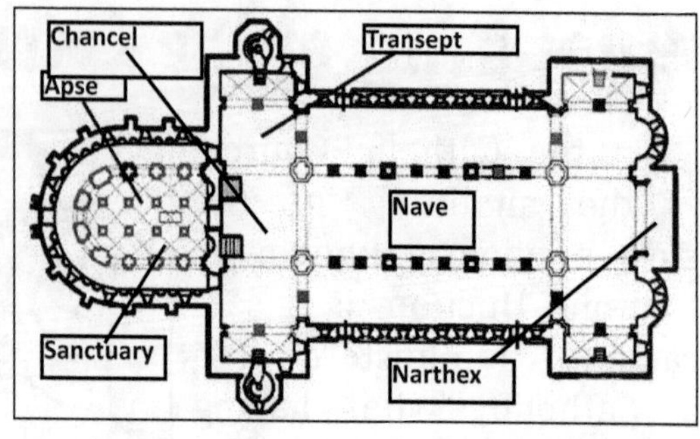

This is the space at the end of a church housing the sanctuary. It is often built as an extension to the main body of the church and can have with a domed or circular roof, and is traditionally at the eastern end of the church.

Apostasy/Apostate

Apostasy is the total rejection of Christianity by a baptised person who, having at one time professed the Christian faith, publicly rejects it. It is distinguished from heresy, which is limited to the rejection of one or more Christian doctrines by one who maintains an overall adherence to Jesus Christ. One who undertakes apostasy is known as an **Apostate**.

Apostle

The word "apostle" originally meant "envoy" or "messenger", and was applied in the New Testament to the group of 12 original followers of Jesus, whom he appointed

explicitly for a particular function in the Church. This group became 11 with the betrayal of Judas, and back to 12 when the remaining Apostles chose Mathias to replace Judas. Their unique place is based not only on having witnessed the resurrection but also on having been commissioned and empowered by the resurrected Lord to proclaim the Gospel to all nations.

Apostolate

An apostolate in the Church is an organisation or institution "directed to serving and evangelising the world". It also refers to a form of evangelistic activity or work; for example, education, healthcare, and so on. The lay apostolate is made up of laypersons, who are neither consecrated Religious nor in Holy Orders, but who exercise a ministry within the Church.

Archbishop/Archdiocese

An Archbishop (or Metropolitan Archbishop) presides over an ecclesiastical Province or Metropolitan area which comprises several dioceses, in addition to his own diocese, known as an Archdiocese. However, the rank of Archbishop can also be conferred in non-Metropolitan Sees, and may also be conferred on a Bishop in his personal capacity (*ad personam*). Archbishops, especially those who work in Church administration or government, or as Nuncios, may also be appointed to "titular Sees" – which are ancient Sees which no longer function as dioceses. (See also "See".)

Ashes (Ash Wednesday)

The practice of marking the forehead with ashes on Ash Wednesday comes from the ancient Jewish tradition of penance and fasting, which included the wearing of ashes on the head. The ashes symbolise the dust from which God made us. As the priest applies the ashes to a person's forehead, he speaks the words: "Remember that you are dust, and to dust you shall return." Alternatively, the priest may speak the words: "Repent and believe in the Gospel."

Ashes also symbolise grief - in this case, grief that we have sinned and caused separation from God. We do not wear ashes to show how holy we are, but to acknowledge that we are sinners. They are a sign of repentance, humility and mortality.

Ashes are traditionally made from the burned palms blessed on the previous year's Palm Sunday.

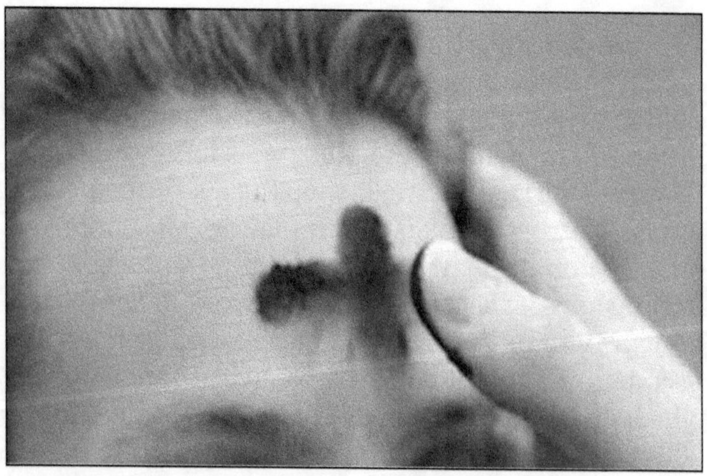

Aspergillum

This an instrument used with an *asperso-rium* (holy water bucket) to sprinkle holy water. Its name comes from the Latin *aspergere* which means *to sprinkle.*

The wand-shaped object (see at right) is used to sprinkle holy water to bless people in the congregation, as well as at Baptisms, to bless candles at Candlemas/palms on Palm Sunday, and to bless a house or sacramental objects, or a coffin at a funeral. Sometimes a priest may use a fresh-cut green branch or a small straw whisk in its place.

Aspersorium

This is a bucket-like basin with a handle for carrying holy water. It is used with the aspergillum during blessings with holy water. Usually, an altar server carries the aspersorium while the priest dispenses holy water with the aspergillum.

Assumption

The Feast of the Assumption (August 15) commemorates the belief that when Mary, the mother of Jesus Christ, died, her body was "assumed" into heaven to be reunited with her soul instead of going through the natural process of physical decay upon death.

B

Baldachin

A baldachin (from Italian *baldacchino*) protects the Blessed Sacrament or sacred relics from the sun or rain during processions. The baldachin can be shaped like an umbrella or a canopy and is carried on poles. A baldachin also refers to the permanent canopy over the main altar in some churches.

Baptismal Font

The water basin or pool where the sacrament of Baptism is administered. Some churches place the baptismal font near the entrance so the faithful may dip their fingers into it and bless themselves, and to emphasise that baptism is the sacrament of entry into the Church. Other parishes place the font closer to the sanctuary or in a separate building or room called a baptistery. In some cases, the Baptismal font is large enough for the total immersion of an adult.

Baptismal Shell

This is a scalloped, shell-like dish used by priests or deacons to pour water over the head of those who are being baptised. The use of a scallop shell in baptism dates from ancient times and may symbolise the beginning of the Christian journey, since the scallop shell is also a symbol of pilgrimage.

Beatification

This is the third of four steps in the process by which a holy person who has died is officially proclaimed to be a saint by the Church. Beatification requires that at least one miracle which has been attributed to the intercession of the candidate for sainthood has been fully certified by the Church. Once beatified, the candidate is given the title "Blessed" (as in Blessed Benedict Daswa).

Beatitudes

The Beatitudes are teachings by Jesus in the Sermon on the Mount in Matthew's Gospel. They describe blessings for qualities valued in Heaven. "Beatitudes"

comes from "beatus," meaning blessed. Each begins with "Blessed are", and highlights a virtue leading to divine favour.

Bells (Altar)

The altar bells are used in the Mass to focus the attention of the congregation on what is about to happen and is happening at the consecration. When you hear the priest say the words of Christ, "This is my Body," and, "This is my Blood" you will usually hear a bell ring. The ringing of this bell, an ancient practice, alerts the congregation that Jesus is present - that the consecration of the bread and wine into the body and blood of Jesus Christ is taking place. There is also a tradition that the bells are rung throughout the Gloria at the Easter Mass of the Resurrection.

Bells (Church)

Church bells in the Christian tradition are bells (or a single bell) usually placed in a tower either attached or separate from the church, and which are rung for a variety of ceremonial purposes. Traditionally they were (and still are) used to call worshippers to the church for a Mass or a service, and to announce times of daily prayer (Liturgy of the Hours, the Angelus and so on). They are also rung on special occasions such as weddings or funerals.

In medieval times, church bells were also rung in times of danger or threat (such as the approach of an enemy) and to announce and celebrate occasions such as the end of a war. Historically, the bells also rang in European cathedrals to indicate that the consecration had taken place and it was proper for the faithful to worship.

Benediction

Benediction has two meanings in the Church: A benediction (Latin *bene* [well] and *dicere* [to speak]) is, firstly, a short invocation for divine help, blessing and guidance, usually at the end of a worship service.

It also refers to a specific Catholic worship service during which the Blessed Sacrament is exposed in a monstrance for veneration by the people. The people are blessed with the monstrance containing the Blessed Sacrament during this service, hence "Benediction".

Bidding Prayers

These are prayers which are said during Mass after the Creed for the needs of the people, the world and the Church. Also referred to as "The prayers of the Faithful".

Biretta

A square, stiff cap with three or four ridges on top. The colour of the biretta shows rank: a cardinal's is red, a bishop's purple. Priests, deacons, and seminarians wear black. The pope and many priests and deacons do not wear one. The biretta is very seldom used today, but it may be seen in period films and television shows such as "Fr Brown".

Bishop

In the Catholic Church, a bishop is an ordained minister who holds the fullness of the sacrament of Holy Orders and is responsible for teaching doctrine, governing Catholics in his jurisdiction, sanctifying the world and representing the Church. A Bishop is in charge of a "Diocese" which is (usually) a geographical area made of local communities (parishes) of the faithful. The Bishop is the superior of all the priests (except those belonging to religious orders) in his diocese, and is the local spiritual leader of all the faithful of his diocese. He can sometimes be assisted by an Auxiliary Bishop, who is an "Assistant Bishop", or in very special circumstances, by a co-adjutor Bishop, who is a "co-Bishop".

Each bishop has a unique crest. The picture shows the crest of Bishop Zungu OFM of Port Elizabeth in South Africa.

Book of the Gospels

This book contains passages from all four Gospel accounts — Matthew, Mark, Luke and John, and is used by the priest or deacon to proclaim or chant the Gospel at Mass. The book is often beautifully decorated and may be carried to the altar in the entrance procession, and then on to the Ambo in the Gospel procession.

Breviary

A breviary is a Liturgical book which contains the prayers used for the Divine Office (Liturgy of the Hours). See also "Divine Office".

Burse

The burse is a square case of about 20cms square made of two pieces of cardboard covered with silk, lined with linen and bound together at three edges. It is used to carry a folded corporal to and from the altar for Mass or Benediction. The use of the burse has largely been discontinued.

C

Canonisation

This is the final step in the official process by which the Church declares a deceased holy person to be a saint, and acknowledges that they can be venerated by the universal Church as "an example of holiness which can be followed with confidence". It requires the attribution of one further miracle after the candidate has been declared "Blessed" through beatification. (See Saint).

Canon Law

Canon Law is a code (Latin: *ius canonicum*) of ecclesiastical laws governing the Catholic Church and regulating its external organisation and government, as well as ordering and directing the activities of Catholics toward the mission of the Church. It was the first modern Western legal system and is the oldest continuously functioning legal system in the West. In the Latin or Western Church, the governing code is the 1983 Code of Canon Law, a revision of the 1917 Code of Canon Law.

Canticle

anticles are poetic hymns that are often sung in religious liturgies. The term is derived from the word "song," and these selections are taken from both the Old and New Testaments of the Bible.

Cantor

cantor or chanter is a person who leads people in singing, or sometimes in prayer. In most modern parishes, the cantor typically sings or chants the Responsorial Psalm.

Cardinal

Cardinal (Latin: *Sanctae Romanae Ecclesiae Cardinalis,* literally "Cardinal of the Holy Roman Church") is a leading bishop and prince of the College of Cardinals in the Catholic Church.

A cardinal's duties include participating in papal consistories, and conclaves when the Holy See is vacant. Most have additional missions, such as leading a diocese or a dicastery (department) of the Roman Curia, the equivalent of the government of the Holy See.

Cassock

Many Catholics (and others) call any long religious robe a cassock, but there are distinct differences in both usage and style between the cassock, the alb and the habit.

The cassock (from the Old French word *cassaque* meaning "long coat") is a long robe usually worn by clergy in a non-liturgical environment.

Prior to Vatican II, the cassock was worn by all clergy as their standard clerical dress and is today still worn by certain traditional congregations as their usual daily attire.

The colour and trim vary with rank: the Pope wears white, cardinals black with scarlet trim, archbishops and bishops black with red trim, while other "ranks" wear plain black. Cassocks are sometimes also worn by seminarians, monks, and laypeople such as altar servers, choir members and liturgical leaders when assisting with the Mass or other services.

Catechesis

Catechesis is the practice of handing on the Faith to children and the formation and instruction of those who already believe. The Greek word *katechesis* means instruction by word of mouth, especially by the use of the question and answer method, and comes from the verb *katechein* which means "to echo back".

This is what happens in every parish when people, particularly children, are taught the fundamentals of the Faith and its practice.

Catechetics

Catechetics is defined in the dictionary as the branch of theology that deals with catechesis. It is the study discipline or the "science" behind catechesis. It is that part of theological training that deals with the imparting of religious knowledge through catechesis and printed catechisms.

Catechism

A Catechism is a book or manual of religious instruction usually arranged in the form of questions and answers and used to instruct the young, to win converts, and to testify to the Faith.

Catechism of the Catholic Church

The Catechism of the Catholic Church is a catechism promulgated for the Catholic Church by Pope John Paul II in 1992. It sums up, in book form, the beliefs of the Catholic faithful and is a major universal catechism of the Church. The Catechism is part of the Church's official teaching in the sense that it was suggested by a Synod of Bishops, requested by the Holy Father, prepared and revised by bishops and promulgated by the Holy Father as part of his ordinary Magisterium. Pope John Paul II ordered the publication of the Catechism by the Apostolic Constitution, *Fidei Depositum*, on October 11, 1992.

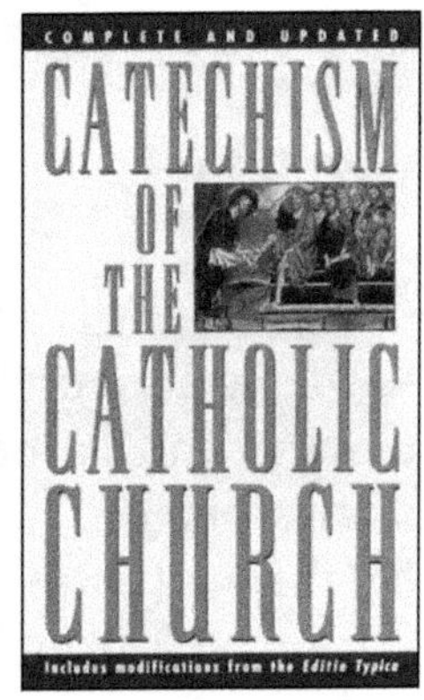

Catechist

The role of a Catholic catechist is to catechise (teach) the Faith of the Catholic Church by both word and example. It has become an extremely important lay ministry in the Church, in the face of declining numbers of priests and religious, who were the traditional catechists.

Catechumen

A Catechumen is defined as a person who is receiving instruction (catechesis) in preparation for Catholic baptism and/or confirmation. The process, as well as the group of people receiving instruction, is known as the "catechumenate".

Cathedral vs Basilica vs Abbey vs Chapel

Cathedral is the central church of a diocese and is the seat of the bishop, housing his throne (Latin *cathedra* = seat/throne).

Contrary to popular perception, a cathedral does not have to be a fancy, expensive or even very large church. It is not about the building, it is about the bishop. Where the bishop is, there is the cathedral.

Basilica: There are two types: basilicas major and basilicas minor. The basilicas major are the four personal churches of the Pope and are in and around Rome: the Archbasilica of St John Lateran, St Peter's Basilica, the Basilica of St Paul Outside the Walls, and the Basilica di Santa Maria Maggiore. Basilicas minor can be found around the world and are awarded that status by the Pope, usually because of some sort of historical, spiritual, or architectural significance. The term "basilica" is an additional label to whatever the structure already is; any cathedral or church can also be a basilica.

Abbey: An abbey is, strictly speaking not a

church, although it always includes a church, but is an enlarged version of a monastery, housing a religious congregation and under the leadership of an Abbot and/or an Abbess.

Chapel: A chapel is a place of worship that has no pastor or priest and no permanent congregation; it's all about the physical space, designed and made available for worship. In the classic sense, it is usually much smaller than a church — sometimes just a room — and can  be within a church itself or in a secular place like a hospital or airport. However, there are some very large and beautiful chapels – such as the Sistine Chapel in the Apostolic Palace in the Vatican, and Sainte-Chapelle in Paris, with its magnificent stained glass windows, which was the chapel of the French royal family.

Celebrant

The person who presides at a religious service is referred to as a celebrant. The celebrant at Mass is always a priest, but other ministers/lay people may be celebrants at other services.

Celibacy

This refers to a decision to live chastely in the unmarried state. At ordination, a diocesan priest or unmarried deacon in the Latin rite Catholic Church makes a promise of celibacy. The promise should not be called a "vow." The adjective is "celibate". See chastity.

Chalice

The chalice occupies the first place among sacred vessels. It is a cup-shaped vessel or goblet used at Mass to contain the Precious Blood of Christ. For centuries it was made of precious material - if it was not of gold, the interior of the cup was gold-plated. Since Vatican II, chalices may be made of other materials. A chalice is consecrated with holy Chrism by a bishop. Traditionally, a chalice could only be handled by a priest or deacon, but that has been relaxed to allow lay Extraordinary Ministers of the Eucharist and Sacristans to do carry out their duties.

Chalice Veil

The Chalice Veil is used to cover the chalice and paten when they are being carried to the altar. Its use is decreasing in many churches.

Chancel

In church architecture, the chancel is the space around the altar, including the choir and the sanctuary, at the liturgical east end of a traditional Christian church building. It may terminate in an apse. It is generally the area used by the clergy and choir during worship, while the congregation is in the nave.

Chancery/Chancellor

Chancery is the traditional name for the administrative offices of a Catholic diocese. It is in the diocesan chancery that, under the direction of the Bishop or his representative, all documents which concern the diocese are drawn up, copied, forwarded, and a record kept of all official writings expedited or received.

The **Chancellor** is the chief archivist of a diocese's official records and is also sometimes a notary and secretary of the diocesan curia, or central administration; he or she may have a variety of other duties as well. It is the highest diocesan position open to women.

Charism

The Catechism of the Catholic Church defines charisms as "graces of the Holy Spirit which directly or indirectly benefit the Church, ordered as they are to her building up, to the good of men, and

to the needs of the world" *(Article 799)*. In everyday language, a charism can be understood as a gift from God that allows a person or group to live out the Gospel in relation to the world around them.

Charismatic Renewal

The Charismatic Renewal in the Catholic Church is a spiritual movement that focuses on a deep relationship with the Holy Spirit, highlighting the many "charisms" that are given to Catholics through the sacraments of baptism and confirmation.

There is an emphasis within the Renewal on a proper discernment of charisms, asking the Holy Spirit to reveal which gifts God has given to them for the overall good of the Church. This is often expressed in "ordinary" charisms, such as the charism of "encouragement," "faith" or "giving." However, the Renewal is most often known by others for certain "extraordinary" charisms that are often visibly seen at charismatic prayer meetings. This would include the charism of "healing," "intercessory prayer" or "speaking in tongues".

It is very important to note that this movement is an integral part of the Catholic Church, and Catholic Charismatics subscribe fully to all the teachings of the Church just as all the faithful do. The movement celebrated its 50th Anniversary in 2017 with Pope Francis in St Peter's Square in Rome.

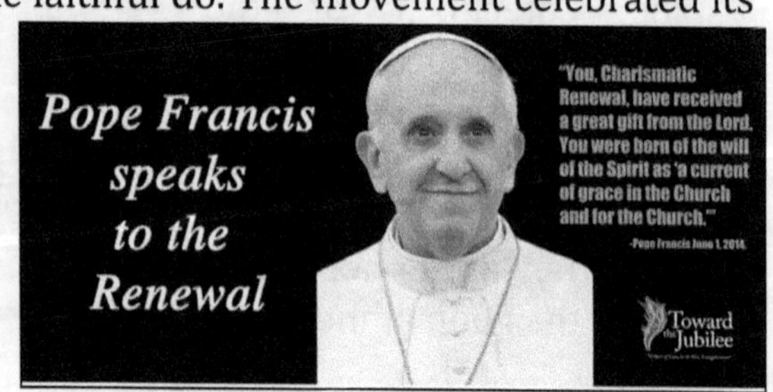

Chastity

In its general sense chastity does not mean abstinence from sexual activity as such, but rather moral sexual conduct. Marital chastity means faithfulness to one's spouse and moral conduct in marital relations. The religious vow of chastity taken by brothers, sisters and priests in religious orders is a religious promise to God to live the virtue of chastity by not marrying and by abstaining from sexual activity. When diocesan priests and unmarried deacons make a promise of celibacy, they are not taking religious vows; their commitment to live chastely in an unmarried state should be described as a promise, not a vow. See celibacy.

Chasuble

This sleeveless outer vestment is worn by the priest over all other garments when he celebrates Mass. The poncho-like garment covers his entire body with only an opening for the head. Historically, it is derived from a garment which protected the wearer from inclement weather. The colour of the chasuble changes for the different seasons of the church year and for special occasions – green (ordinary time), red (Lord's passion, Palm Sunday, Pentecost, martyrs), white (Christmas, Easter, Feasts of the Lord, and at funerals to signify our baptism and Resurrection), violet/purple (Advent, Lent and funerals), rose (Gaudete Sunday).

Choir

By definition, a choir is an organised group of singers, especially one that takes part in church services. Depending on the congregation or church, a choir can be a highly organised group of very talented and proficient singers, who will often perform outside of the church, or a group of volunteers with talent whose primary function is to lead the congregation in singing the hymns and responses of the Mass. In the old days, the choir was not only the people who sang but also a particular place within a church, more often than not in a gallery. Today, in modern churches, the choir usually inhabits a place which is part of the congregation – this is to emphasise our unity and also encourages the rest of the congregation to participate in the singing.

Ciborium

The ciborium is a covered vessel which is used for distributing Holy Communion in churches and for reserving the consecrated hosts in the tabernacle. In shape, the ciborium resembles a chalice, and it is provided with a conical cover surmounted by a cross or some other appropriate device. This vessel is not consecrated but rather blessed, and may be handled by a layperson.

Ciborium Veil

As long as the Blessed Sacrament is reserved in it, the ciborium should be covered with a veil of precious material of white colour.

Cincture

The cincture is a long, rope-like cord with tassels or knots at the end that is tied at the waist over 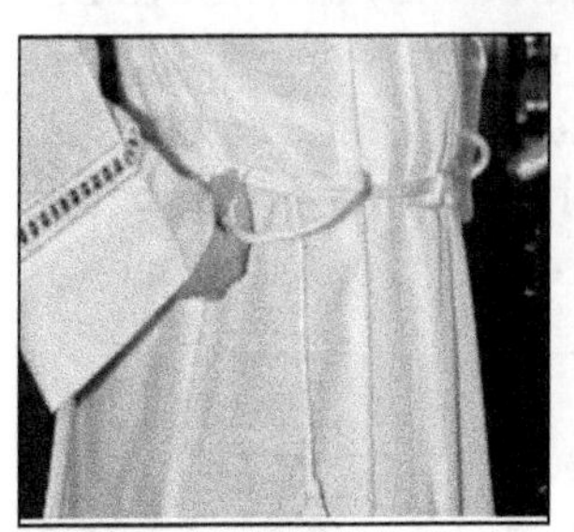 the alb. It is usually white, but the colour may vary according to the liturgical season. The cincture is symbolic of chastity and purity. Cinctures may be worn by priests, deacons and altar servers.

Clergy

This is a term used to refer to the ordained members of the Catholic hierarchy and include deacons, priests, and bishops.

Collect

The Collect is a prayer by the priest which concludes the introductory rite of the Mass. The priest first invites the people to pray. They remain silent for a moment to recall that they are in the presence of God. In the Collect that follows, the special characteristics of the particular Mass are mentioned and these, together with the prayers of the people, are "collected" and are all directed to the Father through Christ and in the Holy Spirit. The people's assent is expressed with an "Amen".

Collection/Offering

During the offertory or immediately before it, a collection of money or other gifts is taken up from the congregation. These may be brought forward together with the bread and wine, but they are not to be placed on the altar. The offering or collection has its Biblical origin in the sacrifices the Jews made to God, as well as the practice of "tithing", in which a proportion of a person's income was given towards the upkeep of the temple.

The money collected is primarily used for the expenses of running the parish.

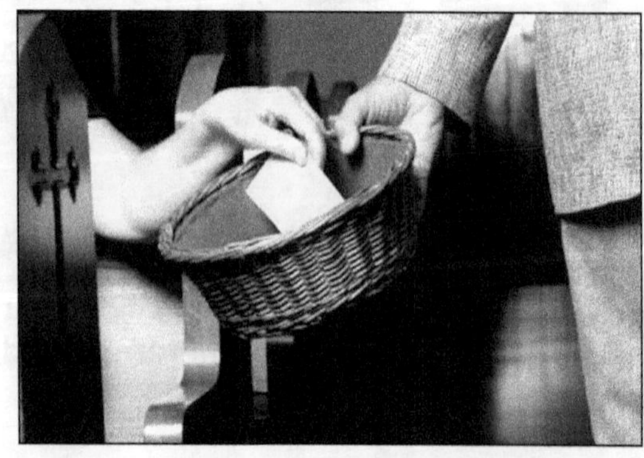

Columbarium

The Columbarium is usually a group of niches, typically within a wall of brick, stone, granite, marble or other materials, which contain the cremated remains (cremains) of the departed. It is a place for the respectful and usually public storage of cinerary urns/ caskets in which the deceased's cremated remains are placed. It obviously also serves as a memorial to the deceased. Columbaria (the plural form) became increasingly prevalent at Catholic Churches after the Vatican lifted the prohibition on cremation in 1963. The Church encourages placement of the cremains in a final resting place, rather than the random disposal of the ashes, hence the Columbarium at churches, which have traditionally been the natural repository and final resting place of deceased members of the Christian community.

Communion under Both Kinds

Receiving Holy Communion in the form of both the Body (bread) and Blood (wine) during Mass is becoming increasingly common in Catholic churches, especially on special occasions.

Concelebration

The celebration of Mass by two or more priests at the same time.

Conclave

A papal conclave is a gathering of the members of the College of Cardinals convened to elect a new bishop of Rome, also known as the pope. The gathering/meeting is held in seclusion.

Confessional/ Reconciliation Room

This is a place designated for priests to administer the Sacrament of Penance or Reconciliation (also known as "Confession"). It may be a box-like structure typically with three compartments separated with screens. The middle compartment is for the priest, and the two side ones have kneelers for those who are confess-ing. Many churches now have a Recon-ciliation Room in which the penitent

may choose between confessing behind a screen or confessing face-to-face in a more relaxed situation, as per the illustration.

Congregation

This is one of those words which has more than one meaning in the context of the Catholic Church.

A Religious Congregation is a type of religious institute or community characterised by its members taking simple vows, whereas members of Religious Orders take solemn vows. These congregations live and work according to a strict set of rules. Members of female congregations are usually referred to as "Sisters" as opposed to "nuns", who take solemn vows.

A congregation is also a group of people assembled for worship purposes. "**Congregants**" are members of that group.

Consecration/Consecrate

The word consecration literally means "association with the sacred". Persons, places, or things can be consecrated, and the term is used in various ways in the Catholic context.

The origin of the word is the Latin stem *consecrat,* which means dedicated, devoted, and sacred.

1. The Consecration is that part of the Mass during

which the bread and wine are consecrated/ changed into the Body and Blood of Christ.
2. Many objects are "consecrated" in the Church: For example, oil (Chrism), patens and chalices, and altars in a new church
3. Traditionally, bishops were "consecrated', but the term "episcopal ordination" is more common these days.
4. People who become brothers and nuns are said to enter "Consecrated Life".

Cope

The cope is a long semi-circular cape, open in the front and reaching down to the ankles. It's fastened at the chest with a clasp. The cope is typically used on ceremonial occasions such as processions, benedictions and Eucharistic adoration. A cope may be worn by a priest, bishop or deacon, and in certain special circumstances, by lay ministers.

Corporal

The corporal is a white linen cloth of about 50 cm square on which the chalice, paten and ciborium are placed on the altar during Mass. During Benediction, the monstrance must also be placed on the corporal. When not in use, the corporal is folded three times each way so as to form nine equal squares and may be placed in a burse. The corporal takes its name from the Latin word *corpus* meaning *body*. Its primary function is to pre-

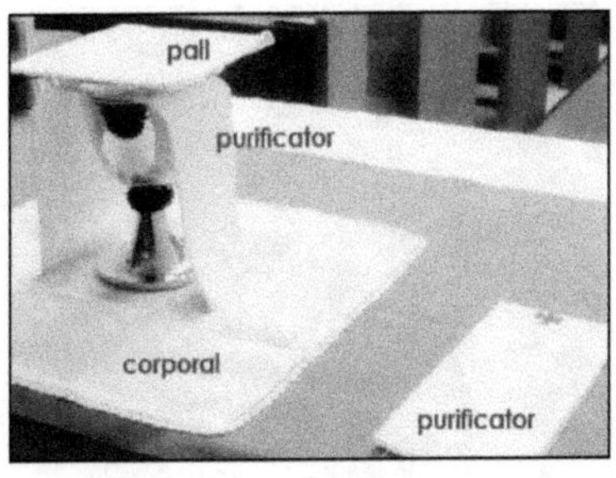

vent fragments of the Blessed Sacrament from being dropped and as it comes into direct contact with the Body and Blood of Christ, has to be treated with respect and reverence. There are certain protocols to be followed for the washing of the corporal.

Credence Table

A credence table is a small table, placed to the side of the altar, which is used to hold the chalice, paten, cruets, lavabo bowl and other liturgical objects when they are not in use.

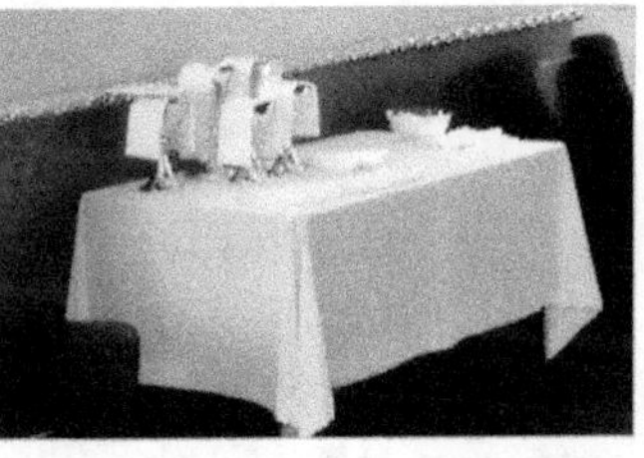

Creed

A Creed is a confession of faith, a symbol, or a statement of faith, as in the Apostles' Creed and the Nicene Creed. The word "Creed" comes from the Latin "Credo", meaning "I Believe," with which the Creed begins. It is a statement and a profession of the shared beliefs of a Church

Crosier

A Crosier is an ornamental staff shaped like a shepherd's crook that is carried by bishops and abbots as a symbol of their office. The hook is meant to "pull back" the straying sheep of the bishop's flock symbolically, while the pointed end is to encourage the reluctant sheep. A bishop typically holds the crosier with his left hand so he can bestow blessings with his right.

Crotalus

This is a wooden clapper that is used in place of bells during the 48-hours between the Holy Thursday Eucharist and the Easter Vigil. That time marks the period of the Passion of Christ when the bells of the church remain silent. While few parishes still use it, many, if not most monasteries, still do. The crotalus calls the brothers to pray the Liturgy of the Hours during that period.

Crucifix

The crucifix is a cross to which is attached a sculpted or painted image of Jesus' body. Its purpose is to remind us of the suffering of Christ on the Cross. Wherever Mass is celebrated, a crucifix must be visible. Most churches have one behind or over the altar. A crucifix is also attached to the pendant part of all rosaries. A crucifix is also often worn as jewellery around the neck, and is displayed on the wall of Catholic homes.

Crucifix (Processional)

The Processional Crucifix is a crucifix mounted on a pole of about 2 m long. It is usually carried at the front of the procession that enters the church at the beginning of Mass, and also during the exit procession at the end of Mass. By the way, the cross-bearer is called the **"Crucifer"**.

Cruets

These are small jars, often with stoppers, that contain the water and wine used during Mass. They are typically made of glass so that the water and wine can easily be distinguished. If they are made of metal, a V (*Vinum - Wine*) or an A (*Aqua - Water*) is inscribed to identify the contents.

Curia (Roman)

The Roman Curia comprises the administrative institutions of the Holy See and is the central body through which the affairs of the Catholic Church are conducted. It is made up of several secretariats and dicasteries (departments).

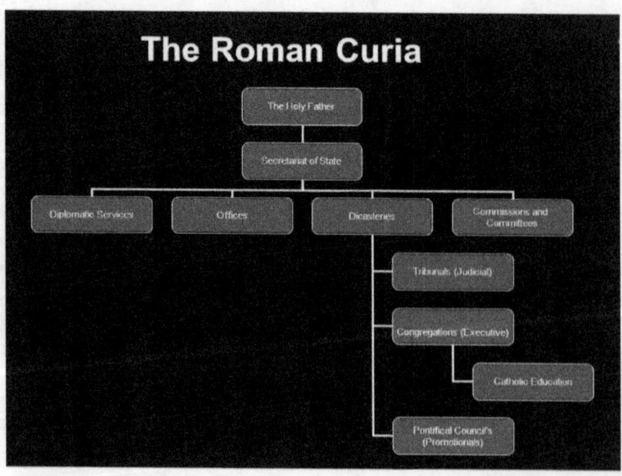

Dalmatic

A Dalmatic is an outer vestment, worn by a deacon, with short open sleeves, an opening for the head, and open at the sides from the hem to the shoulders, reaching just below the knees. The deacon wears it during Mass, especially at solemn liturgies like the Sundays of Advent, Lent, Easter, Christmas and Solemnities. The colour of the dalmatic matches the chasuble worn by the priest and corresponds to the liturgical season.

Deacon

In the clerical hierarchy of the Catholic Church, the pope is at the top, then cardinals, bishops, priests, and then deacons. Catholics recognise two types of deacons:

Permanent deacons are men ordained to this office who normally have no intention or desire to become priests. They can be single or married. If the latter, they must have been married before being ordained deacons. If a deacon's wife dies before him, he may be ordained a priest, if the bishop permits and approves. Under normal circumstances, a deacon is not permitted to re-marry if his wife passes away. Permanent deacons, especially those who are married, have secular jobs to support their families. They help the local pastor by visiting the sick, teaching the Faith, counselling couples and individuals, working on parish committees and councils, and giving advice to the pastor.

Transitional deacons are seminarians, students in the last phase of training for the Catholic priesthood. After having been a deacon for a year and after fulfilling all other criteria, they can be ordained a priest by the bishop. Deacons can baptise, witness marriages, perform funeral and burial services outside of Mass, distribute Holy Communion, and preach. They are obligated to pray the Divine Office (Breviary) each day.

Deanery/Dean

A Deanery is a regional group of parishes within a diocese under the care of a dean, who is usually one of the pastors of those parishes. The word "dean" is derived from the Latin *decanus*, a leader of ten people. The purpose of this arrangement is to assist the bishop in the administration of the diocese. The Deanery will typically deal with local issues affecting its parishes.

Dedication

Dedication in the Catholic sense is the act of consecration of a church for use as a place of worship and the celebration of the Eucharist and other sacraments. The Dedication of the church usually also includes the Dedication of the Altar. Dedication can also be used in other scenarios, such the Dedication of a country to Our Lady.

Deuterocanonical Books

"Deuterocanonical", meaning "of or pertaining to a second canon". This term refers to the seven additional books in the Old Testament (and two additions - to *Esther* and *Daniel*) that the Catholic Church

believes are part of the canon of Scripture inspired by the Holy Spirit. These books are: *Tobias, Judith, Baruch, Ecclesiasticus, Wisdom, First* and *Second Maccabees.* Also known as the "**Apocrypha**" or "**Apocryphal Books**".

Dicastery

A Dicastery is a department of the Roman Curia, the administration of the Holy See through which the pope directs the Roman

Catholic Church. A Dicastery is equivalent to a Ministry in secular government.

Diocese

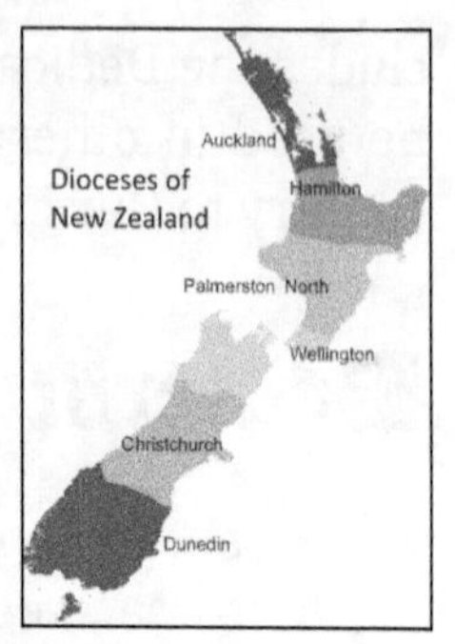

group of church communities, usually in a given geographical area under the supervision of a bishop, is known as a diocese. Typically, a diocese is divided into parishes which are each overseen by a priest. A diocese headed by an Archbishop is known as an **Archdiocese**.

Diocesan/Secular Priests

diocesan or secular priest is under the authority of his diocesan bishop. He will generally only work/minister within that geographical diocese, usually as a parish pastor or in diocesan administration, or in a diocesan ministry like hospital or prison chaplaincy or in education. Unlike his counterparts in the various Religious Orders and Congregations, the diocesan priest is not required to make a vow of poverty.

Discernment

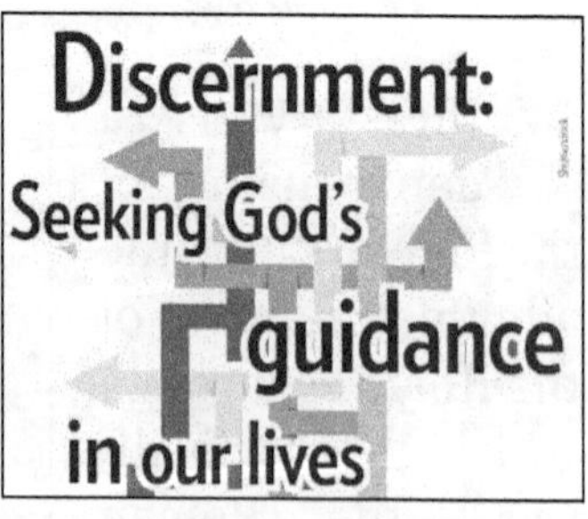

ocational discernment is the process by which men or women in the Catholic Church "discern", or recognise, their vocation in the church. The vocations are life as a layperson in the world, either married or single, or the ordained life, or the consecrated life.

Divine Office/Liturgy of the Hours

The Divine Office (Latin: *Officium Divinum*), the Liturgy of the Hours (Latin: *Liturgia Horarum*) or Work of God (Latin: *Opus Dei*) or canonical hours, contained in a Breviary, is the official set of prayers "marking the hours of each day and sanctifying the day with prayer".

It consists primarily of psalms supplemented by hymns, readings and other prayers and antiphons. Together with the Mass, it constitutes the official public prayer life of the Church. Celebration of the Liturgy of the Hours is an obligation undertaken by priests and deacons intending to become priests, while permanent deacons are only obliged to recite a part. See also Breviary.

Dispensation

This is Exemption from a Church law in a particular case for a special reason. For example, people over a certain age may be exempted from Fasting and Abstinence.

Doctors/Fathers of the Church

Doctor of the Church (Latin *doctor* "teacher") is a title given by the Catholic Church to saints recognised as having made a significant contribution to theology or doctrine through their research, study, or writing.

They form a part of the magisterium (authentic teaching authority) of the Roman Catholic Church. Among these doctors of the Church are: St Augustine (*pictured*), St Gregory the Great, St John Chrysostom, St Therese of Lisieux and St Ambrose.

The Church Fathers, Early Church Fathers, or Fathers of the Church were ancient and influential Christian theologians and writers who established the intellectual and doctrinal foundations of Christianity. There is no definitive list, but they do include some of those known also as Doctors of the Church. The historical period during which they flourished is referred to by scholars as the Patristic Era, ending approximately around AD 700.

The Apostolic Fathers were Christian theologians who lived in the 1st and 2nd centuries AD, who are believed to have personally known some of the Twelve Apostles, or to have been significantly influenced by them. The first three are considered the chief ones: Clement, Ignatius and Polycarp.

Doctrine vs Dogma

In general, doctrine is all Church teaching in matters of faith and morals. **Dogma** is more narrowly defined as that part of doctrine which has been divinely revealed and which the Church has formally defined and declared to be believed as revealed.

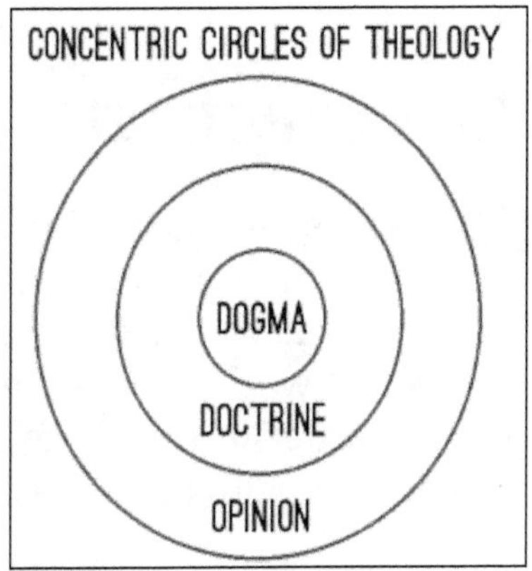

Doxology

Glory Be

Glory be to the Father,
and to the Son,
and to the Holy Spirit,
as it was in the beginning,
is now, and ever
shall be, world
without end.

Amen.

Christian prayer which gives praise and glory to God, often in a special way, to the Three Divine Persons of the Trinity. One common Doxology in the Mass is the *Gloria*. Another is the little *Glory Be* we pray in the Rosary.

E

Ecclesiastical

This adjective means "anything relating or pertaining to the the Church". Pews, readings from the Bible, and stained glass windows are all part of the ecclesiastical world. The ecclesiastical hierarchy is the pecking order of the clergy, and high-ranking clergy are considered to be "ecclesiastical authorities".

Ecumenical Council

This is a gathering of all the bishops of the world, in the exercise of their collegial authority over the universal Church. An Ecumenical Council is usually called by the successor of St Peter, the Pope, or at least confirmed or accepted by him.

Ecumenism

The term ecumenism refers to efforts by Christians of different church traditions to develop closer relationships and better understandings. The term is also often used to refer to efforts towards the visible

and organic unity of various Christian denominations in some form. The adjective "ecumenical" can also be applied to any interdenominational initiative that encourages greater cooperation between Christians and their churches, whether or not the specific aim of that effort is full, visible unity.

Encyclical

This is a pastoral letter which is written by the Pope and published to outline Church teaching on a particular issue. Pope Francis has produced three to date, *Lumen Fidei* (The Light of Faith) , *Laudato Si'* (Praise Be to You) and *Fratelli Tutti* (All Brothers).

Episcopal

This word means "of or relating to a bishop", as in Episcopal See (Diocese).

Epistle

From the Greek word meaning "letter". In the Christian context, this word refers to one of the 21 books in the New Testament that were written,

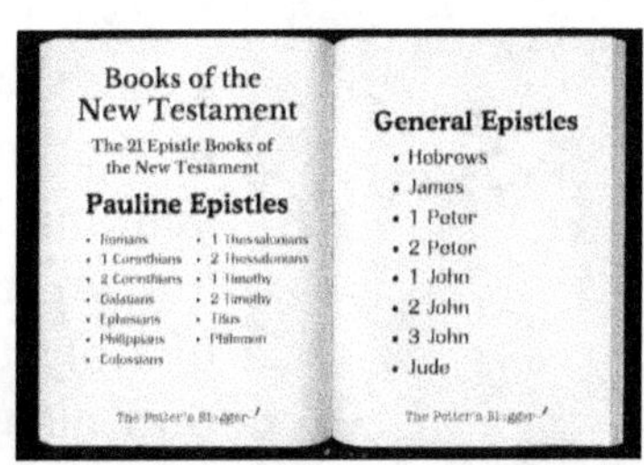

mostly by Apostles (the author of the Letter to the Hebrews is "unknown"), as letters to instruct and encourage the members of the early Church.

Eremitical Life

The life of a hermit, separate from the world in praise of God and for the salvation of the world, in the silence of solitude, assiduous prayer, and penance.

Eschatology

From the Greek word "eschaton", meaning "last." Eschatology refers to the area of Christian faith which is concerned about "the last things," and the coming of Jesus on "the last day": our human destiny, death, judgement, resurrection of the body, heaven, purgatory, and hell, all of which are contained in the final articles of the Creed.

Eucharistic Ministers

Unordained parishioners who are chosen by the parish to assist the priest in the distribution of the Body and Blood of Christ at communion time during Mass. Also known as Extraordinary Ministers of Holy Communion. These ministers also routinely administer the

Eucharist to parishioners who are housebound or in hospital

Evangelise/Evangelisation

To preach and spread the Gospel in such a way that it brings about repentance, conversion, transformation and salvation, and brings others to Christ and his Church. In the words of Pope Paul VI, "Evangelising means to bring the Good News into all the strata of humanity, and through its influence transforming humanity from within and making it new." *Evangelii Nuntiandi, 18).*

Evangelist

The four Evangelists - the four authors who are credited with the writing of the Gospels - Matthew, Mark, Luke, and John. The term is also used to describe someone who works actively to spread and promote the Christian faith.

Examen

The daily Examen is a technique of prayerful reflection on the events of the day in order to detect God's presence and discern his direction for us. The Daily Examen came to us from St Ignatius of Loyola in his "Spiritual Exercises".

Examination of Conscience

Prayerful self-reflection on our words and deeds in the light of the Gospel to determine how we may have sinned against God. One ought to prepare for the reception of the Sacrament of Reconciliation by such an examination of conscience.

Excommunication

A severe ecclesiastical penalty resulting from grave crimes against the Catholic religion, imposed by ecclesiastical authority or incurred as a direct result of the commission of an offence. Excommunication excludes the offender from taking part in the Eucharist or other sacraments and from the exercise of any ecclesiastical office, ministry, or function.

Exorcism

Exorcism is the religious practice of evicting evil spirits from a person or place. The phrase itself is most commonly associated with Christianity, specifically Catholicism, and is the public and authoritative

act of the Church to pro-
tect or liberate a person
or object from the pow-
er of the devil (demonic
possession) in the name
of Christ.

Expiation

The act of redemption and atonement for sin im-
plies an attempt to undo the wrong one has done,
either by suffering a penalty or making reparation.

Exposition

The Exposition of the Blessed Sacrament is the act
of exposing the Eucharist to the faithful, usually
in association with Benediction or Adoration.

F

Faculties

In the Catholic Church, a faculty is "the authority, privilege, or permission, to perform an act or function". The most common use of the term is in the context of "priestly faculties", which is the permission given to a priest by his diocesan bishop or religious superior, legally permitting him to perform the Sacraments. Normally, a priest's faculties only permit him to celebrate within his own diocese or religious institute. This also applies to deacons.

Faith (The Faith)

Catholic Faith is defined as the sum of truths revealed by God in Scripture and tradition and which the Church presents in a brief form in its creeds. According to St Thomas Aquinas, faith is "the act of the intellect assenting to a Divine truth owing to the movement of the will, which is itself moved by the grace of God".

Faithful (The Faithful)

This term is used to refer to those who have been joined with Christ in Baptism and have become the people of God, the Church. See also "Laity/Lay People".

Faith Formation

Catholic Faith Formation refers to the ongoing education, particularly of adults, in all aspects of the Faith. It also refers to the specific education of those destined for particular ministries. Faith Formation also applies the ongoing education of Religious and Clergy.

Faldstool

A portable backless ceremonial chair used by the bishop when celebrating Mass away from his cathedral. It may also be used for support when kneeling. The seat is made of cloth  or leather and may have a cushion whose colour corresponds to the liturgy season. It is believed to have originated from the camp stool the bishop would use when he travelled throughout his diocese to visit parishes.

Fast/Fasting

The Church has des-ignated certain days (Ash Wednesday and Good Friday) as days of fasting and abstinence. In the Catholic context, fasting is defined as having one full meal and two smaller meals (which together make up one meal) in the course of the day. The rules of fasting apply to people between the ages of 18 and 59.

Feast vs Solemnity vs Memorial

Catholics commonly use the word "feast" to cover everything from the celebration of various saints' days to major celebrations such as days dedicated to Our Lady, as well as such celebrations as Corpus Christi. However, strictly speaking, these celebrations are divided into Solemnities, Feasts and Memorials. The difference is primarily in the importance of the day, and there are minor differences in Liturgy.

A **Solemnity** is a feast day of the highest rank, celebrating a mystery of Faith such as the Trinity, an event in the life of Jesus, his mother Mary, or other important saint. Solemnities include the celebrations of Christmas, Easter, the Annunciation of the Lord, Pentecost, Ascension, Assumption and so on. If a Solemnity falls on a Sunday, its celebration and liturgy replaces that of the Mass of the Day.

Feasts are next in importance and honour a mystery or title of the Lord, of Our Lady, or of saints of particular importance (such as the Apostles and Evangelists).

Memorials are usually of saints but may also celebrate some aspect of the Lord or of Mary. Examples include the optional memorial of the Holy Name of Jesus or the obligatory memorial of the Immaculate Heart of Mary. In certain circumstances, a feast and/or memorial may be elevated to a solemnity - for example, in Ireland, the feast of St Patrick, who is the country's patron saint, would be celebrated as a solemnity, whereas elsewhere it would be a memorial.

Fraction Rite

The "Fraction Rite" may be an unfamiliar term for many people. However, almost all would recognise this part of the Mass by the "Lamb of God" litany that accompanies it.

The name "Fraction Rite" comes from the focus of this rite: the breaking of the sacred Host. This action symbolises Christ's body broken for us, so that when we receive Holy Communion, we may be one, united in Christ.

Gifts of the Holy Spirit

The traditional list of seven gifts of the Spirit is derived from Isaiah 11:1-3: wisdom, understanding, knowledge, counsel, piety, fortitude, and fear of the Lord.

Gluttony

Overindulgence in food or drink. Gluttony is one of the seven capital sins.

Grace

In the definition of the Catechism of the Catholic Church, "grace is favour, the free and undeserved help that God gives us to respond to his call to become children of God, adoptive sons, partakers of the divine nature and of eternal life".

Grace is what is given to us by God so that we might attain eternal life; it is impossible for us to attain eternal life apart from God's grace, and it is solely due to God's grace that we can be saved and enter into Heaven. There are two kinds of grace that a given person can receive. One is called "Actual" Grace. The other kind of grace is called "Sanctifying" Grace.

Among the principal means of grace are the sacraments (especially the Eucharist), prayers and good works. The sacramentals also are means of grace.

Grace - State of

This is commonly defined as the condition of a person who is free from mortal sin and pleasing to God. It is the state of being in God's friendship and the necessary condition of the soul at death in order to attain heaven.

Grace - at Meals

Grace at meal-times is a short prayer or thankful phrase said before or after eating. It is also a request for a blessing on the food and those present. Reciting such a prayer is referred to as "saying grace".

The term comes from the Ecclesiastical Latin phrase *gratiarum actio*, "act of thanks". The act of saying grace is derived from the Bible, in which Jesus and Saint Paul pray before meals (*cf. Luke 24:30, Acts 27:35*). The practice reflects the belief that humans should thank God who is the origin of everything.

Grotto

A grotto, in the Catholic sense, is a structure which is built to resemble a cave, and into which is usually placed a statue of Our Lady. The tradition of housing the statue of Our Lady in a "grotto" stems from the apparition of Our Lady to St Bernadette in a cave at Lourdes in France in 1858. Grottoes are often built in the grounds of churches, convents, schools, institutions and other areas of religious significance.

H

Habit

A religious habit is a distinctive set of religious clothing worn by members of a religious order and applies to both men and women. Habits can vary greatly according to the particular order, but usually consist of

a long tunic or cassock-like garment, a scapular with or without a cowl and/or a cloak or hood for men, and cowl and/or cloak and veil for nuns.

Heresy/Heretic

Heresy has a very specific meaning in the Catholic Church. Anyone who, after receiving baptism and while professing to remain nominally a Christian, emphatically and continuously denies or doubts any of the truths that must be believed with Divine and Catholic faith, is considered a heretic, and subject to excommunication. A heretic would also be one who actively promotes a doctrine or belief which is contrary to that of the Catholic Faith.

Hermit

One who lives the eremitical life. Through silence and solitude, in prayer and penance, the hermit vows, although not necessarily publicly, to follow the evangelical counsels out of love for God and desire for the salvation of the world.

Holy Days of Obligation

These are principal feast days on which, in addition to Sundays, Catholics are obliged by Church law to participate in the Eucharist.

Holy Eucharist vs Holy Communion vs Holy Mass

Many Catholics, especially in modern times, blur the lines of distinction between the Holy Eucharist, Holy Communion and the Holy Sacrifice of the Mass. The Holy Eucharist, Holy Communion and Mass are connected, but they are not same thing.

The Eucharist is the name of the Sacrament of Christ's Body and Blood. There are seven Sacraments in the Church, the most blessed of which is the Sacrament of the Eucharist. The word "eucharist" comes from a Greek word meaning "thanksgiving". However, the "thanksgiving" we are speaking of is a very specific thanksgiving. It is the thanksgiving for Christ's sacrifice for us which makes present to us his person, his Body and Blood. Thus, since this is not any "thanks-

giving" but this specific "thanksgiving" we do not call this Sacrament "Eucharist", we call it "the Eucharist" (or "the Holy Eucharist", or "the Most Blessed Sacrament of the Eucharist").

But isn't **Holy Communion** also the Eucharist? The answer is no. Holy Communion is something more specific: it the reception of the Eucharist. The Eucharist in its ministration to the faithful is called "Holy Communion."

Holy Mass. From the Latin word *missa*, Mass is the name we use to describe the celebration of the Sacrament of the Eucharist. The gathering of the faithful during which the Eucharist is consecrated at the altar and distributed to the faithful as Holy Communion is called Mass. Mass requires the proper minister (Bishop, priest) to be celebrating, the proper offerings (bread, wine), the intention of the Church and the use of the proper Ritual.

Holy Oils

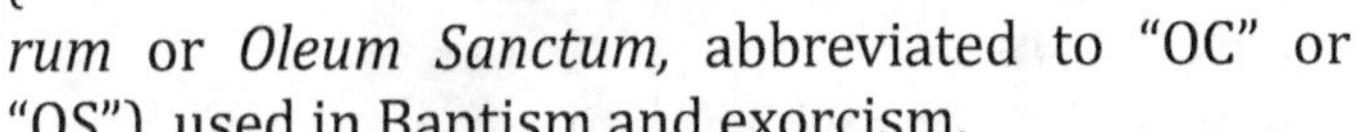

Three different kinds of holy oils are used in the administration of sacraments:

- The Oil of Catechumens *(Oleum Catechumeno- rum* or *Oleum Sanctum,* abbreviated to "OC" or "OS"), used in Baptism and exorcism.
- The Holy Chrism *(Sanctum Chrisma,* abbreviated to "SC") is used in the anointing after Baptism, at Confirmation, the conferring of Holy Orders and the Consecration of churches.
- The Oil of the Sick *(Oleum Infirmorum,* abbreviated to "OI"): used in the anointing of the sick or when praying for the sick and laying hands on them at healing services.

These oils are usually blessed by the bishop on Holy Thursday at what is known as the Chrism Mass, and are kept in an ambry. They are often in glass vessels inscribed with the abbreviation of the oils to identify them.

Holy Oil Stock

These are small containers used to store the three kinds of holy oils that will be used during the administration of the sacraments. When not being used, the stocks are stored in the ambry. The Oil of the Sick is often transported in a stock when a priest visits a sick person and anoints him or her outside of a church.

Holy Orders/Ordination

Holy Orders is the sacrament by which bishops, priests and deacons are ordained and receive the power and grace to perform their sacred duties.

The sacred rite by which orders are conferred is called **Ordination**. The Apostles were ordained by Jesus at the Last Supper so that others could share in his priesthood.

The Rites of Ordination occur during Mass after the Gospel. The minister of Holy Orders is a validly ordained bishop.

Holy Water Font

These are small containers that are filled with holy water – that is, water that has been blessed. They may be free-standing or attached to the wall, usually near the doors of churches so that people may dip their fingers and bless themselves when entering and leaving — a baptismal reminder.

Homily vs Sermon

The words **homily** and **sermon** are often used interchangeably, but there is a slight difference between them. A homily is commentary delivered by a priest or deacon after the reading of scripture. The subject of the homily is the scripture that has been proclaimed during the religious service. It is a discussion of the chosen passage/s from the Bible. In fact, the word homily is derived from the Greek word *homilia*, which means conversation.

A **sermon** is a speech or discourse on religion or morals. A sermon may be in reference to a scripture that has been proclaimed during the service, but it may also sim-

ply be a topic on religion or morals that the speaker chooses to explore. Sermons may also be offered outside of religious services or may be published as a text. Sermon is derived from the Latin word *sermonem* which means speech or discourse.

Host

A small, thin, round, unleavened wafer made of wheat flour, which is consecrated and consumed at Mass. Before consecration, the Host is simply a

piece of flattened bread but, after the words of consecration are spoken by the priest, the Host is the Body of Christ, in which He is really present.

Hymns

The sacred songs sung at Mass and other celebrations, defined as "Religious songs or poems, typically in praise of God."

Hymnal

This is the book that contains the words and music for the hymns that are sung at Mass. Hymnals are typically found on a rack at the back of each pew. Hymnals have, to a large extent, been replaced by overhead or data projectors, which project the words of the hymns on to a screen or a wall. However, most churches will retain a supply of hymnals as a backup in case of technical or power failure.

Humeral Veil

The humeral veil consists of a piece of cloth of about 2,75 m long and 90 cm wide; generally of embroidered and decorated silk or cloth of gold, which is draped over the shoulders and down the front.

At the ends, there are sometimes pockets in the back for hands to go into so that the wearer can hold items without touching them directly with the hands.

The humeral veil is most often seen during the

liturgy of Exposition and Benediction of the Blessed Sacrament. When priests or deacons bless the people with the monstrance, they cover their hands with the ends of the veil so that their hands do not touch the monstrance as a mark of respect for the sacred vessel and the Blessed Sacrament it contains. This is to emphasise that it is Jesus present in the Eucharistic species who blesses the people and not the minister.

The humeral veil is also seen at the Mass of the Lord's Supper. It is used when the Ciborium containing the Blessed Sacrament is taken in procession to the Altar of Repose, and again when it is brought back to the altar without solemnity during the Good Friday service.

I

Immaculate Conception

This is the dogma proclaimed in Christian Tradition and defined in 1854, that from the first moment of her conception, Mary by the singular grace of God and by virtue of the merits of Jesus Christ was preserved immune from original sin. The dogma that states that Mary, whose conception was brought about the normal way, was conceived without original sin or its stain. That's what "immaculate" means: without stain.

Imprimatur

The Latin term for "let it be printed," which signifies the approval by a Catholic bishop for a religious work to be published.

Incardination

Priests and deacons in the Catholic Church must be attached to a particular diocese or religious institute to which they must be accountable and which must be accountable to them. Every cleric in the Church makes a promise or vow of obedience to a bishop, prelate or religious superior, who directs his ministry and ensures that he is engaged in the work of the Gospel in accordance with his talents, aptitudes and abilities. The superior is, at the same time, responsible for ensuring that the cleric receives lodging, food, healthcare, and remuneration for his pastoral work. No priest or deacon can function in the Catholic Church if he is not accountable to a superior.

This relationship of obedience and accountability between a cleric and his diocese or religious order is referred to as <u>incardination</u>. The word literally means "to be hinged" because a cleric is attached as if by a hinge. Typically, incardination is a life-long relationship.

Incarnation

Incarnation is the fact that the Son of God assumed human nature and became man in order to accomplish our salvation in that same human nature. Jesus Christ, the Son of God, the second Person of the Trinity, is both true God and true man, not part God and part man. The Incarnation is the mystery and the dogma of the Word made Flesh.

Incense/Incensing

Incense consists of grains or powder consisting of a variety of spices and aromatics, including frankincense, myrrh and copal.

The incense is placed into a thurible containing burning charcoal, and it releases an aromatic smoke. The thurible is then closed, and taken by the chain and swung by the priest, deacon or server or acolyte towards what or who is being "censed". Incensing

is sometimes used to bless and purify the altar, the ministers and the people at Mass, as well as the casket at a funeral and the monstrance during Benediction. There are two symbolic purposes:

Firstly, the rising smoke of the incense symbolises the prayers of the faithful rising to heaven. Secondly, incense has been used as part of sacrifice and offerings since ancient times. (See Thurible).

Incense Boat

A small container in which the incense is kept before use. From there, it will be spooned into the thurible by the bishop, priest or deacon for burning. (See Thurible).

Indulgence

In the teaching of the Catholic Church, an indulgence (Latin: *indulgentia*, from *indulgeō* - permit) is "a way to reduce the amount of punishment one has to undergo for sins". The recipient of an indulgence must perform an action to receive it. This is most often the saying (once, or many times) of a specified prayer, but may also include the visiting of a particular place or the performance of specific good works. The practice of granting indulgences was commercialised and abused in the Middle Ages and was the target of reformers such as Martin Luther. The granting of indulgences has been drastically reformed in recent times.

There are two kinds of indulgences: partial and plenary. A partial indulgences removes part of the temporal punishment due for sins. A plenary indulgence removes all of it.

Infallibility

Papal infallibility is a dogma of the Catholic Church that states that, in virtue of the promise of Jesus to Peter, the pope when appealing to his highest authority is preserved from the possibility of error on doctrine "initially given to the apostolic Church and handed down in Scripture and tradition". Infallibility is only conferred on papal pronouncements which are solemnly and dogmatically defined, and does not apply to remarks by the pope as a private indiviual, and only when speaks "ex cathedra" (from the chair).

Intercession

A form of prayer - Intercessory Prayer - of petition on behalf of others. The prayer of intercession leads us to pray as Christ, our unique Intercessor, prayed. (See "Prayers of the Faithful").

K

Kerygma

The act of proclaiming or the core message proclaimed, of the Good News of salvation through Jesus Christ. Kerygma is a Greek word used in the New Testament for "proclamation". Amongst biblical scholars, the term has come to mean the core of the early Church's oral tradition about Jesus. Pronounced *ki-rig-muh*.

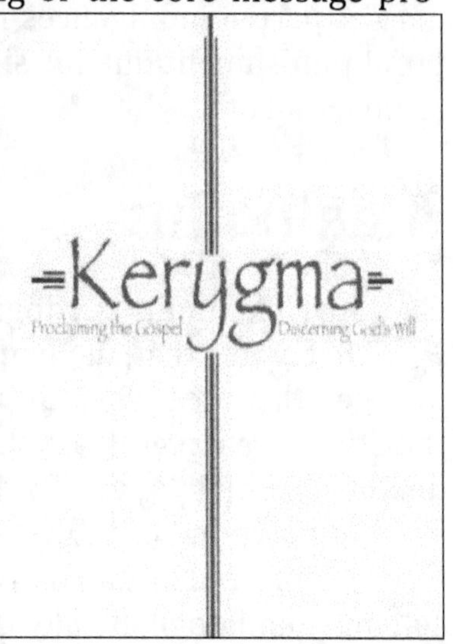

Kyrie Eleison/Christe Eleison

Greek words meaning: "Lord have mercy/Christ have mercy". Sometimes said or sung in Greek during the penitential rite of the Mass.

L

Lavabo/Lavabo Set

Lavabo is the ceremonial washing of the hands in the liturgy. A lavabo set includes a vessel for water and a dish. At Mass, the priest washes his hands after the offertory. He, or the altar server, pours water over his hands and uses the dish to catch the water.  Some sets also include a lavabo towel for drying the hands. The word *lavabo* means *I shall wash* in Latin.

Laity/Lay people

The body of worshippers, as distinguished from the clergy.

As defined by Vatican II:

The term laity is here understood to mean all the faithful except those in Holy Orders and those in the state of religious life specially approved by the Church. These faithful are by baptism made one body with Christ and are constituted among the People of God; they are in their own way made sharers in the priestly, prophetical, and kingly functions of Christ; and they carry out for their own part the mission of the whole Christian people in the Church and in the world.

Lay Ministry/Minister

The Church calls people to the responsible stewardship of their time and talents in support of the Church. This often takes the form of volunteering for a specific lay ministry, most of which are liturgical, catechetical, or involved in pastoral care and social justice.

Liturgical lay ministries include lectors/proclaimers (Ministers of the Word) who proclaim scriptural passages during the Mass, altar servers and acolytes who assist the presider at the altar, cantors and music ministers who lead the singing, Extraordinary Ministers of Holy Communion who assist with the distribution of communion during Mass and/or take Holy Communion to the sick and homebound, ushers or Ministers of Hospitality who direct the seating and procession of the assembly, and Sacristans who prepare for the Mass and look after linens, vestments and sacred vessels. Catechetical lay ministries include Catechists, retreat leaders and youth group leaders. Other lay ministries include those who work with charitable activities, pastoral care and outreach, or advocacy for social justice.

Lectionary

The Lectionary is the book containing the Scripture readings used during Mass. There are three lectionaries: Volume I is for weekday Masses (sometimes spilt into two books), Volume II for Sunday Masses and feasts, and Volume III for Votive and Ritual Masses and special occasions.

The Catholic Lectionary originated in the early Church, where it generally went by the Latin name *Ordo Lectionum Missae.*

The Lectionary for Sundays generally organises the scripture passages to be read in Masses as follows: a reading from the Old Testament; a Responsorial Psalm; a reading from one of the Letters (Epistles) or the Acts; a reading from one of the Gospels. The Lectionary is organised into a three-year cycle of readings. The reading cycle is denoted by letter as *A, B,* or *C.* The year A cycle begins at the Advent near the end of those years whose number is evenly divisible by 3 - 2019. There is also a two-year cycle for the weekday readings (Year 1 and Year 2). Weekday readings are organised as follows: a reading from the Old Testament OR the Letters, a Responsorial Psalm, and a reading from one of the Gospels.

Litany

A Litany is a form of prayer used in services and processions and consists of several petitions by the leader with alternate responses by the congregation. The word comes through Latin *litania,* which is from the Ancient Greek *litaneía,* which in turn comes from *litê,* meaning "supplication". One of the most familiar Litanies is the Litany of the Saints. The "Lamb of God" in Mass is also a Litany.

Liturgy

Liturgy comes from the Greek word, *leitourgia*, literally meaning "the people's work". In the Catholic Church it is used to describe all public acts of worship that take place, as it draws the people into the work of God. It is through the liturgy that people engage with the faith and deepen their relationship with God. Liturgy is the divine worship of the Church and includes the celebration of Mass, the celebration of the Sacraments, and the Divine Office or Daily Prayer of the Church.

Liturgical Year

The celebration throughout the year of the mysteries of the Lord's birth, life, death, and Resurrection in such a way that the entire year becomes a "year of the Lord's grace." Thus the cycle of the liturgical year and the great feasts constitute the basic rhythm of the Christian's life of prayer, with its focal point at Easter.

Lunette

The lunette is a circular container used to hold the host in place when it is placed in the monstrance for exposition. Lunettes are usually made of gold, or are gold plated.

ℳ

Magisterium

One of the most misunderstood and misused words associated with the Church is the Latin term *magisterium*. Many people seem to think that the Magisterium is a "who": the Pope, for example, or the Pope and the world's bishops, or the Pope and the Curia in Rome. Magisterium is a "what", not a "who." It is "the teaching authority of the Church". "The Church" is more than its episcopal leadership. Papal statements which teach on a matter of faith and morals are called magisterial pronouncements and are binding on Catholics. The teachings and writings of the Church Doctors and Fathers are also considered part of the Magesterium.

Martyr

The Greek word "martus" means a witness who testifies to a fact of which he has knowledge from personal observation. In Christian terms, the word came to be exclusively applied to a witness to the truth of the faith, in which the martyr endures even death to be faithful to Christ.

Picture shows the martyrdom of St Stephen - the first Christian martyr.

Mass Intention

A Mass Intention means that the sacrifice of the Mass is offered for some person(s) living or dead. An individual may ask a priest to offer a Mass for several reasons: for example, in thanksgiving, for the intentions of another person (such as on a birthday), or, as is most common, for the repose of the soul of someone who has died. It is common practice that a stipend or small payment is given to the priest for Mass Intentions, although this is not obligatory, and may be waived by the priest. The origins of this practice date back to the early Church and its importance is clearly recognised. When we face the death of someone, to have a Mass offered for the repose of his/her soul and to offer our prayers is more beneficial and comforting than any sympathy card or bouquet of flowers. To have a Mass offered on the occasion of a birthday, anniversary or special need is appropriate, beneficial and appreciated.

Minister

In the Catholic Church the term "minister" enjoys a variety of usages. It most commonly refers to the person, whether lay or ordained, who is commissioned to perform some act on behalf of the Church - Extraordinary Minister of the Eucharist.

On the other hand, to Minister to people in the Catholic sense is to provide for their needs, mostly spiritual, but in some cases, also physical needs. As it has been defined: To render aid or a service for the greater good and salvation of the people.

Missal (Roman)

The Roman Missal is the book containing the prescribed prayers, chants, and instructions for the celebration of Mass in the Catholic Church, and is intended primarily for the use of the congregants. It is usually available in two versions: The Daily Missal, which contains the prayers, readings and liturgy for every day of the year, and the Sunday Missal, for use on Sundays and major feasts.

Missal Stand

This is a book stand with a slanted top used to hold the Sacramentary — the book containing the prayers of the Mass — in a convenient position for the celebrant during Mass so that he can read it when standing at the altar.

Mission/Missionary

This is another of those words which have multiple meanings in the Catholic Church. In the first instance, we speak of the Church's Mission: To carry out and continue the work of Jesus Christ on Earth. "You will be my witnesses in Jerusalem, throughout Judea and Samaria, and to the ends of the earth" (*Acts 1:8*). The Mission of Jesus to proclaim the Kingdom of

God to all people has been handed onto the Church and individual believers, guided by the Holy Spirit.

The Church carries its mission out in a number of ways:

First, there is the Pastoral Mission which is the ongoing work to build up the members of the Church. This work can include the familiar "Parish Mission", a time set aside in the life of a Parish for renewal and deepening of faith, usually conducted by visiting preachers. These are "home missions" geared toward Catholics, distinguished from apostolic missions to make conversions among non-believers.

Second, there is the Mission to the ends of the earth, literally and metaphorically, where the Gospel of Jesus is shared. This can mean travelling to remote and/or troubled areas to bring the Gospel. "Missions" or outposts are established and staffed by "Missionaries", which can include preachers, teachers and medical practitioners. These outposts need not be only in far and remote countries, but also in communities in where special needs are discerned. An example could be the Missions to Sailors and Seafarers.

Finally, there is the Mission of the new evangelisation. This is the attempt to reach out to those who may have faded from the Church or become separated for any number of reasons.

Picture shows Mass in a simple early Mission church in Musina, South Africa. 

Mitre

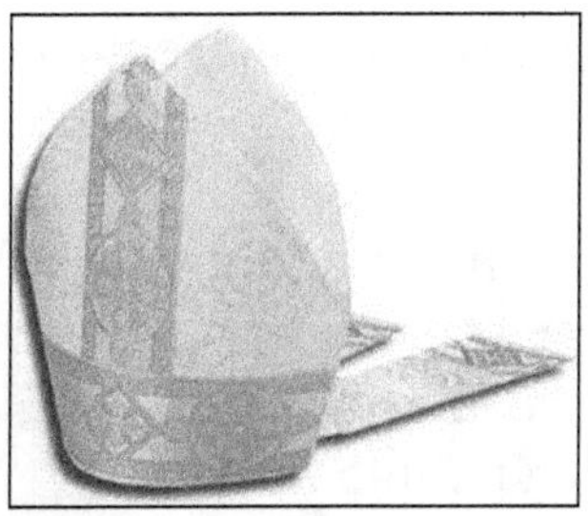

A mitre (or miter) is the tall hat that the bishop wears for ceremonies. It consists of two equal cone-shaped parts that rise up to a peak. The two parts are joined at the base by a cap of soft material so that it can be folded flat. It has two decorative flaps attached to the brim that hang down the back. The mitre is worn over a zucchetto.

The mitre is worn when the bishop is seated, when he gives the homily, when he greets the people, addresses them, or gives the invitation to prayer, when he gives a solemn blessing to the people, when he confers a sacrament, and when he is walking in procession.

Monks vs Friars vs Brothers

A **Monk** may conveniently be defined as a member of a community of men, leading a more or less contemplative (monastic) life apart from the world, under the vows of poverty, chastity, and obedience, according to rules characteristic of the particular order to which he belongs. Monks may be priests or lay brothers. Typical monastic Orders include the Benedictines, Cistercians, Trappists and Carthusians.

<u>**Friars**</u> are different from monks in that they are called to live in service to society, rather than through cloistered asceticism and devotion. Friars work among laypeople and are supported by donations or other charitable support. The word "friar" is from the Middle Ages French term

fraire, which means "brother." The word arose with the creation of the mendicant (travelling/preaching) Orders in the late Middle Ages, most predominantly by Saint Francis of Assisi (*Franciscans - pictured here*) and Saint Dominic (Order of Preachers, or "Dominicans"). These "new religious" were no longer tied to monasteries and convents but went out among the people, to preach and to pray, to educate and to serve the sick.

A Catholic Lay <u>**Brother**</u>, or simply Brother, is someone who is a member of a Religious Order, and who is not a priest and does not plan on becoming a priest. A Brother fulfills a role more focused around manual service and secular matters, as opposed to the more spiritual and pastoral work of the ordained clergy. Brothers can be found in most of the major Orders and are subject to the same vows of poverty, chastity and obedience as priests. There are also Orders that consist almost exclusively of Brothers, and these most often specialise in specific areas of ministry such as education, healthcare and so on. Most Catholics encounter Brothers in the area of education, with well-known teaching Orders such as the Christian Brothers,

Marist Brothers and Brothers of Charity (pictured).

Monsignor

The title of "Monsignor" in the Catholic Church signifies a priest who has distinguished himself and has been honoured by the Pope for his service to the Church, usually at the request of a bishop. The title is an honorary one and is not a specific rank in the Church hierarchy. Soon after his election in March 2013, Pope Francis suspended the granting of the honorific title of Monsignor except to members of the Holy See's diplomatic service.

Monstrance

This has been described as a "Very Catholic thing"! The monstrance (also called an *ostensorium*) is the sacred vessel used for presenting the Body of Christ (in the form of a consecrated host) for Adoration or to carry it in procession. The monstrance is usually made of gold or silver and often has radiating "rays" around the centre. The Host can be seen at the centre of the monstrance behind clear glass. The word monstrance comes from the Latin word *monstrare,* which means *to show.* The priest or deacon should not touch the monstrance directly when it contains a consecrated host. He should place his hands inside a humeral veil to handle it.

Mozzetta

The mozzetta is a short cape that covers the shoulders to the elbow. The colour of the mozzetta represents the rank of the person wearing it:

- Priests who are rectors of parishes: Black mozzetta
- Rectors of basilicas: Black mozzetta with red piping and buttons.
- Bishops: Violet mozzetta.
- Cardinals: Scarlet mozzetta.
- Pope: Can wear five different coloured mozzettas, depending on the season.

Narthex (Foyer)

A place for the people of the congregation to gather and welcome, and forms the entrance and exit of the building. It represents the transition from the secular to the sacred and is a place of respect and silence where all are equal. (See also Apse).

Nave

The "body" of the church, or the central and principal part of a Christian church, extending from the entrance (the narthex) to the transepts (transverse aisle crossing the nave in front of the sanctuary in a cruciform church) or, in the absence of transepts, to the chancel (the area around the altar). The nave is where the people sit, stand or kneel during prayer, Mass and other services. See also Apse.

New Covenant

The new "dispensation," order or Covenant, established by God in Jesus Christ, to succeed and perfect the Old Covenant of the Old Testament.

Nihil Obstat

A Nihil Obstat ("nothing hinders") is a certificate granted by a person, usually a cleric appointed by the bishop, which says there is no objection to the publication of a document pertaining to the Church.

Novena

A novena (from Latin: *novem* - nine) is an ancient tradition of devotional praying in the Church, consisting of private or public prayers repeated for nine successive days or weeks. Novenas are often prayed in preparation for a feast day or for a specific intention. Novenas may be prayed individually or in a group, even if physically separated.

Novice

A person who has been accepted into a religious order and who is undergoing a period of training , discernment and formation before taking vows.

Novitiate/Novitiate House

The period a novice spends in training, and the place where it happens.

Nuncio

An Apostolic Nuncio (also known as a Papal Nuncio or simply as a Nuncio) is an ecclesiastical diplomat of the Holy See to a State or to an international organisation. A Nuncio is appointed by and represents the Holy See, and is the head of a diplomatic mission, called an *Apostolic Nunciature*, which is the equivalent of an embassy. A Nuncio is usually an archbishop. In addition, the Nuncio serves as the liaison between the Holy See and the Church in that particular nation, working with the local Council of Bishops. He plays an important role in the selection of bishops. Pictured here is the Papal Nuncio to New Zealand, Archbishop Rugambwa.

Nun vs Sister

These are two common terms often miunderstood and/or misused by Catholics. This confusion is made worse by the fact that a nun is usually addressed as "Sister". Most people use the term "nuns" to refer to both nuns and sisters, but there are some significant differences. Nuns' lives are spent in prayer and work within their convent or monastery, and are members of an "enclosed" or "cloistered" order.

Sisters are more active in the world, engaging in many different kinds of work, most often for people who are in great need.

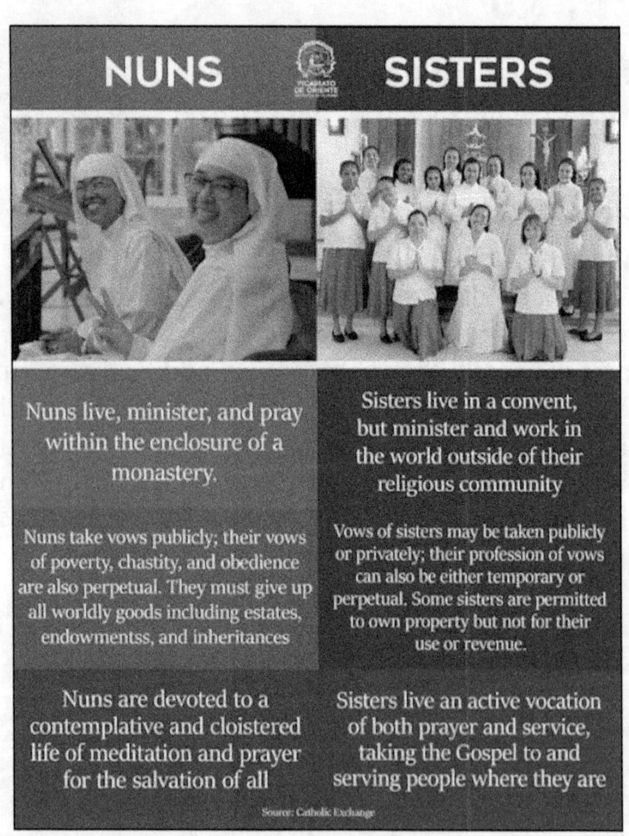

Obligation (Holy Days)

In the Catholic Church, Holy Days of Obligation are days on which the faithful are expected to attend Mass, and engage in rest from work and recreation, according to the Third Commandment. According to Canon Law: *Can. 1246. §1. Sunday, on which by apostolic tradition the paschal mystery is celebrated, must be observed in the universal Church as the primordial holy day of obligation. The following days must also be observed: the Nativity of our Lord Jesus Christ, the Epiphany, the Ascension, the Body and Blood of Christ, Holy Mary the Mother of God, her Immaculate Conception, her Assumption, Saint Joseph, Saint Peter and Saint Paul the Apostles, and All Saints. §2. With the prior approval of the Apostolic See, however, the conference of bishops can suppress some of the holy days of obligation or transfer them to a Sunday.*

Oratory

As a general term, "Oratory" means a place of prayer, but in the Catholic context, it specifically refers to a structure other than a parish church, set aside by the Church authority for prayer and the cele-bration of Mass. It may be public, semi-public, or private and not in-tended for the use of the general public, with spe-cific rules governing its use in each of those settings. It is also used in the names of specific Religious congre-gations such as the Congregation of the Oratory of St Philip Neri. Picture shows the Oratory of St Philip Neri in Birmingham, England.

Order, Religious

In the Catholic Church, a Religious Order is a type of religious community characterised by its members professing solemn vows and an adherence to a specific set of rules. Religious Orders can contain monks, priests and brothers for men, and female members of such Orders are usually called nuns and/ or sisters. There are also Orders exclusively for nuns.

Ordinary

The word "Ordinary" has several meanings in the Catholic context:

1.   The **Ordinary,** or the Local Ordinary - A Bishop or Archbishop is the Ordinary of a diocese, and the major superior is the Ordinary of a religious institute or society of apostolic life. Bishops and major superiors are called Ordinaries because they have what is called "Ordinary Powers" to make and enforce laws. (Picture: Archbishop Paul Martin of Wellington, New Zealand).

2. The Mass of Paul VI that was introduced in 1969 was called the **Ordinary** Form (OF) of the Mass by Pope Benedict XVI in *Summorum Pontificum*, meaning that it is the "usual" form of the Mass that is celebrated in the Catholic Church. Pope Benedict used "Extraordinary Form" to refer to the Mass of Saint John XXIII according to the Missal of 1962, which is celebrated less often. The Mass of 1962 is what is commonly called the traditional Latin Mass.

3. **<u>Ordinary</u>** Time, meaning ordered or numbered time, is a total of 33 or 34 weeks, divided into two parts of the liturgical year. The first part of Ordinary Time is from the Monday following the Feast of the Baptism of Our Lord up to Ash

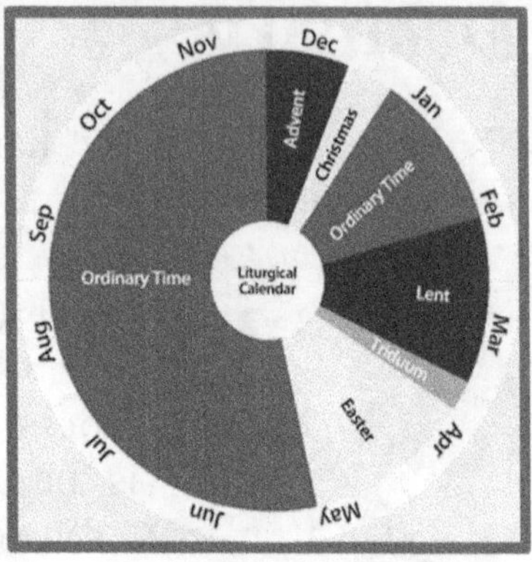

Wednesday, and the second part is from Pentecost Monday to the First Sunday of Advent. The Liturgical Colour for this season is green.

4. Bishops, priests, and deacons are the **<u>Ordinary</u>** (usual) Ministers of the Eucharist, in contrast to Extraordinary Ministers, who are usually lay people or Religious.

5. Parts of the Mass that generally do not change are called the **<u>Ordinary</u>**. The parts that do change are called the Proper or Propers of the Mass, and refer to the particular Mass of the day.

Ordination

Ordination is the rite of the Sacrament of Holy Orders by which the bishop, through the imposition of hands and the prayer of consecration, confers the order of bishop, priest, or deacon to exercise a sacred power which comes from Christ on behalf of the Church.

Original Sin

Original sin is a Christian belief in a state of sin in which we have existed since the fall of humanity, stemming from Adam and Eve's rebellion in Eden, namely the sin of disobedience. The Church teaches that we are all born with the stain of original sin.

Orthodox Churches

The Orthodox Churches are a communion of Churches in schism from the Vatican - they do not recognise the authority of the pope - but retaining valid sacraments and Apostolic Succession. That is to say, if a Catholic had no other option they could receive the Eucharist or be absolved in Confession by an Orthodox Priest.They are in an imperfect but deep communion with the Catholic Church by reason of our common Baptism, the profession of the Creed, and the possession of true sacraments by reason of the apostolic succession of their priesthood.

Picture: Pope Francis meets Orthodox Patriarch Bartholomew

P

Pall

Pall is a stiffened square card covered with white linen, usually embroidered with a cross or some other appropriate symbol. The purpose of this pall is to keep dust and insects from falling into the Eucharistic elements in the chalice.

Pall (Funeral)

A pall (also called mortcloth or casket saddle) is a cloth that covers a casket or coffin at funerals. The word comes from the Latin *pallium* (cloak). The derivation is the same for both Palls: they are named after the cloth that covered the body of Jesus.

Pallium

The pallium is a white, woollen band with pendants in the front and in the back worn around the neck and shoulders over the chasuble. Seen from the back, it resembles the capital letter Y. It is said to represent Christ the Good Shepherd, who carried the lost sheep on his shoulders. Only the Pope and archbishops wear the pallium. It has been the tradition for the pope to bestow the pallium on metropolitan arch-

bishops (those who oversee dioceses or archdioceses that are the largest in their Church province) annually on the feast of Sts Peter and Paul, on June 29.

Palm Branches

On Palm Sunday of the Lord's Passion, palm branches are blessed as Mass begins. On that day, the faithful attending Mass wave the branches as the priest and other attendants enter the church. This recalls

the entry of Christ into Jerusalem when the crowds met him cheering "Hosanna" and waving palm branches to honour him. The palms blessed at this Mass are retained in people's homes through the year and are brought back the following year to be burned to provide the ashes for Ash Wednesday.

Parables

A characteristic feature of the teaching of Jesus. A parable is a short and simple story that teaches a religious or moral lesson. The parables of the *Good Samaritan* (shown here) and the *Prodigal Son* are just two examples of the many parables of Jesus, as recorded in the four Gospels.

Paraclete

The Paraclete is a name for the Holy Spirit. It is a Christian biblical term occurring five times in the Gospel and Letters of St John in the New Testament. Paraclete is translated as 'advocate', 'counsellor' or 'helper'.

Paschal Lamb

The Paschal Lamb in Old Testament terms was the lamb sacrificed by the Jews at the feast of the Passover, commemorating the deliverance of the Jewish people from death by the blood of the lamb sprinkled on the doorposts in Egypt, which the angel of death saw and "passed over." St Paul, drawing a parallel with the sacrifice made by Jesus on the Cross, referred to Christ as the "Paschal Lamb" (*I Corinthi-*

ans 5:7); leading to the Christian view of Christ as the spotless Lamb of God who by his death freed mankind from the bonds of sin .

Paschal Candle

The Paschal Candle (or the Easter Candle) is a large, white candle made of beeswax. A new Paschal Candle is blessed and lit from the new Easter fire every year at the Easter Vigil — the night before Easter Sunday. - during a special liturgy called the Service of Light. Various symbols are inscribed on the candle, as explained in the diagram. The candle is then carried into a darkened church to symbolise the arrival of the Light of Christ into a world darkened by the crucifixion.

It is used during the Easter season and throughout the year on special occasions such as baptisms and funerals.

The Easter candle should be placed in close proximity to the Ambo when it is carried into the church – for two reasons: the practical one is to provide light for the Deacon to proclaim the Exultet and the Gospel in a dark church, and the symbolic one is to associate the light of Christ with His Word.

Pastor

In the Catholic Church a pastor is an ordained priest appointed by the bishop to take charge of a Parish, and lead its pastoral care. Also referred to as the Parish Priest or Priest-in-Charge.

Patriarch

A title given to those ancestors or fathers of the Semitic peoples: Abraham, Isaac, and Jacob, who received God's promises. In the Churches of the East, a patriarch is a senior bishop with jurisdiction over a larger unit of particular churches, or patriarchate, of a certain rite or region or liturgical tradition.

Paten

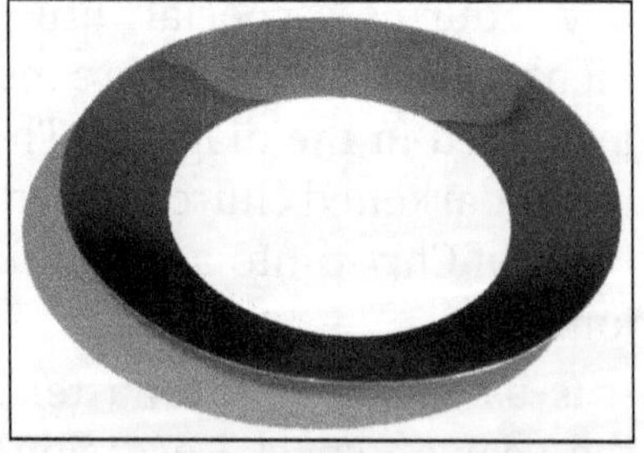

The paten is a plate-like dish on which the priest's hosts are placed during the Mass, before and after the Consecration. The paten can also have a slightly bowl-like shape. It has a very practical purpose: to hold the fragmented host and to prevent any accidental desecration after the Fraction has occurred. Like the Chalice, the paten is consecrated, and strictly speaking, may not be handled by a layperson. However, since the introduction of Extraordinary Ministers of the Eucharist, this has been relaxed to enable them to carry out their duties. Sacristans are usually also given dispensation to handle these sacred vessels

Pentateuch

The first five books of the Old Testament: Genesis, Exodus, Leviticus, Numbers, and Deuteronomy.

Pentecost

The holy day of Pentecost, which is celebrated 50 days after Easter Sunday, commemorates the descent of the Holy Spirit upon the Apostles and other followers of Jesus Christ while they were in Jerusalem celebrating the Feast of Weeks (*Shavuot*), as described in the Acts of the Apostles. The term Pentecost comes from the Greek *Pentēkostē* meaning "fiftieth".

Pew

A long bench with a back on which the members of the congregation can

sit. Pews are aligned to face the main altar in a church. They often have a rack to hold hymnals and missals, as well as kneelers so that the faithful can kneel comfortably, rather than on the floor.

Penance

This is an action which expresses contrition for a sin following forgiveness (absolution) by a priest in the Sacrament of Reconciliation. Penance is usually a prayer or series of prayers but may require a specific act of reparation(such as returning stolen goods).

Pilgrimage

A pilgrimage is a journey, often to the holy places associated with special religious events or holy people, undertaken for personal spiritual or physical reasons (such as healing), or simply as an act of devotion. The person undertaking such a journey is called a pilgrim.

Pontiff

The word "pontiff", or "Holy Pontiff" refers to the pope, and is derived from the Latin *Pontifex Maximus* - literally the "greatest priest or chief high priest" - a title also bestowed on the pope. It was adopted from the ancient Roman religion, and in the latter years of the Roman Empire, was a title given to the Roman Emperors.

Popular Devotions

These are non-liturgical prayers such as the rosary, the Stations of the Cross, litanies, and novenas.

Postulant

A person who has applied to join a religious order and is waiting to be admitted.

Preach

To preach is to deliver a sermon or religious address, and to proclaim or expound the Gospel, usually in a church from a pulpit or ambo.

Presbytery

Presbytery is commonly used in the Catholic Church to denote a clergy house, especially the home of one or more priests. It is also another (mostly not in use) name for the sanctuary in a church. The word derives from the Greek "presbyteros", which means elder or senior.

Presider's Chair

This is the chair on which the priest sits during Mass.

It is placed in the sanctuary of the church and should be turned to face the people. The chair symbolises the importance of the role of the priest as leader of the community's prayer. The picture shows a presider's chair hand made by a parishioner from a large piece of driftwood - Church of St Francis of Assisi, Humansdorp, South Africa.

Proclaimer/Lector

A Proclaimer is a Lay person who has been trained for, and commissioned as a "Minster of the Proclamation of the Word". They are assigned to read the first and second readings at Sunday Mass, as well as the Psalm in the absence of a Cantor.

Proclaimers are competent readers who love the Word of God and make it come alive in the liturgy. They know that people come to the Eucharist to hear sacred scripture and to be inspired by it. They are aware that they must proclaim effectively if God's people are to understand the homily. Above all they know it is God who speaks when they proclaim.

These Ministers used to be called simply "readers" but proclaiming the Word of the Lord goes far beyond merely reading the words in the book.

Proclaimers are also sometimes called Lectors. This is a Latin word meaning "one who reads". The Lector used to be one of the so-called "Minor Orders". These were the steps to the priesthood, which were largely discontinued after Vatican II.

Profession

The taking of vows on joining a religious order.

Profession of Faith

Reciting the creed - "the symbol of faith" - is the Profession of Faith. It summarises the faith professed by Christians. See also "Creed".

Pulpit

The word pulpit stems from the Latin *pulpitum*, and was originally used to denote a theatrical stage. In medieval churches it became a platform primarily used for preaching.  The pulpit was located in the center of the nave (the place where the people stood) and was highly elevated to allow the priest to adequately address his congregation. The pulpit has to a large extent been replaced by the lectern-like ambo, and is usually only found in older churches. The picture shows St Mary's Cathedral, Cape Town, with the pulpit and its canopy on the left.

Purificator

The purificator is the white linen cloth used to purify the chalice and other vessels after the celebration of the Eucharist. Purificators are also used to wipe the edge of the chalice after each person receives the Precious Blood when it is offered.

Pyx

The word pyx most often refers to a small, round container with a lid which is used to carry the Eucharist to the homebound or those in hospitals. However, any vessel that carries the Eucharist may also be called a pyx.

A larger version of the pyx (also called a *Custodia*) is used for the storage in the tabernacle of the larger host used in the monstrance - if it can hold the lunette this pyx is also called a Luna Holder (left).

R

Real Presence

The Catholic Church believes in the doctrine of the Real Presence in the Eucharist, which teaches that during the celebration of the Mass, the bread and wine used in the sacrament of the Eucharist become the actual body and blood of Jesus Christ.

Reconciliation, Sacrament of

Reconciliation (also called the Sacrament of Penance, and commonly known as Confession) is a Sacrament instituted by Jesus Christ in his love and mercy to offer us forgiveness for the times we have sinned and turned away from God. There are four

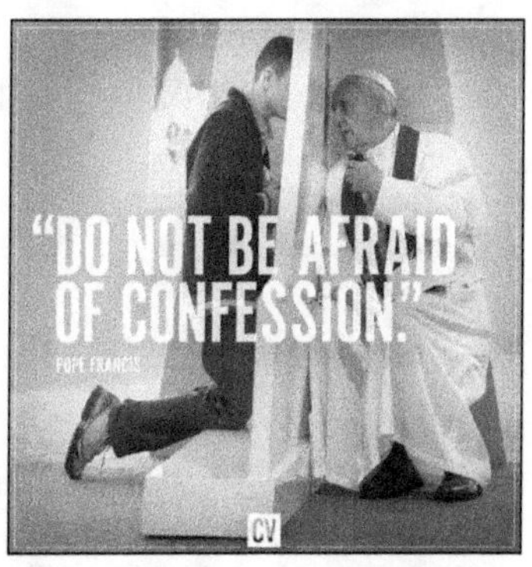

primary actions in the celebration of the Sacrament of Reconciliation, all of which contribute in some way to the healing that takes place: confession of sin; expression of contrition or sorrow for sin; doing penance ("satisfaction"), which expresses a desire to avoid sin; and absolution from sin.

Relic/Reliquary

A relic can be the remains of a saint — such as bones — or something that belonged to a saint, like pieces of clothing. Every Catholic altar will have a relic within it -

originating from the days when the early Christians celebrated Mass in the Catacombs.

A **reliquary** is a container or case in which relics are kept. Reliquaries are often beautifully decorated and vary in size according to the size of the relic.

Religious

A "Religious" (using the word as a noun) is, in the terminology of the Catholic Church, what in common language one would sometimes call a "brother", "monk" or "nun", as opposed to an ordained priest.

More precisely, a Religious is a member of a religious order or religious institute, someone who belongs to "a society in which members pronounce public vows and lead a life of brothers or sisters in common".

Remission of Sins

The forgiveness of sins, which is accomplished in us through faith and Baptism, as the result of the redemptive sacrifice of Christ on the cross. Christ gave the power to remit sins to his Apostles, and through them to the ministers of the Church. The remission of sins committed after Baptism is effected sacramentally through the Sacrament of Penance and Reconciliation.

Requiem Mass

A funeral Mass for the dead. It takes its name from the first word of the prayer with which Mass begins. In Latin this is: "Requiem aeternam dona eis, Domine."(Eternal rest grant unto them, O Lord).

Rite

Like so many words in this book, "rite" has different meanings in different contexts in the Catholic Church.

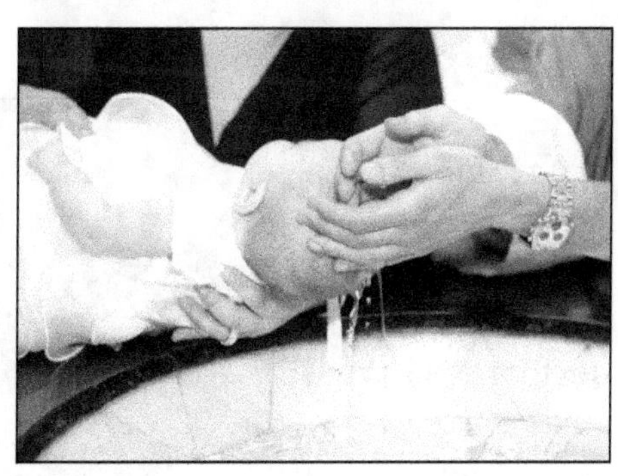

In first instance a rite is a religious or solemn ceremony or act, a customary procedure or observation during the liturgical celebration (for example, the Rite of Baptism).

In the broader context a rite represents an ecclesiastical tradition about how the sacraments are to be celebrated. This refers to the different ways the different branches of the Catholic Church approach the sacraments. You therefore have Latin Rites, Maronite Rites, Armenian Rites and so on.

Rite of Christian Initiation of Adults (RCIA)

The process by which a non-baptised person is prepared to become a full member of the Church is called the catechumenate, which was restored in the Latin Church by the Second Vatican Council, and whose distinct stages and rites are found in the Rite of Christian Initiation of Adults. The foundations of every Christian life laid by the Sacraments of Baptism, Confirmation, and Eucharist, which are the culmination of the RCIA journey.

Ritual

A ritual is a a religious or solemn ceremony or action performed in a customary way according to a prescribed order.

As an adjective, ritual means "conforming to religious rites," which are the sacred, customary ways of celebrating a religion.

Rosary

The rosary is a traditional prayer that originated in the Middle Ages consisting primarily of five sequences of 10 Hail Marys (called "decades" from the Latin *de-*

cem - ten) usually said using a string of beads, also called a rosary, to count the prayers. During each set of 50 Hail Marys, it is customary to meditate on either the *Joyful, Sorrowful, Glorious* or *Luminous Mysteries.*

Each mystery recalls events in the lives of Jesus and Mary. The string of beads used to pray the rosary is also referred to as a *rosary.*

Rubrics

Rubrics are a set of instructions or rules — in the Catholic context, these are the instructions in the Roman Missal printed in red to signal to the priest what he is to **DO**, as opposed to the black ink, which tells him what he is to **SAY**. The word derived from the Latin *rubrica* meaning "red soil". Red soil was used in the medieval Church to make red ink.

Sacramental

Like many words, Sacramental has more than one meaning in the Catholic context. It is used as an adjective and as a noun.

As an adjective, sacramental means "of or pertaining to the sacraments", as in "sacramental wine".

As a noun, a sacramental is a material object, thing or action *(sacramentalia)* set apart or blessed to manifest the respect due to the Sacraments and so to excite pious thoughts and to increase devotion to God.

Holy water, for example, is a sacramental that believers use to recall their baptism; other common sacramentals include blessed candles, blessed palms, blessed ashes, a cross or crucifix necklace, blessed salt, and holy cards, as well as Christian art and icons, especially a crucifix or cross.

Blessings, dedications and consecrations, as well as exorcisms, are also sacramentals.

Sacramentary/Missal

This is the book which contains all the prayers, chants and instructions (or rubrics – printed in red) for the celebration of the Mass by the priest. It contains the general prayers common to all Masses, as well as the specific ones for every day, such as the daily introductory prayers and final prayers.

Sacraments

These are the seven sacraments (or ceremonies) that mark Catholics' religious development through life. They are Baptism, Eucharist (Communion), Reconciliation (Confession), Confirmation, Marriage, Holy Orders and the Anointing of the Sick. They are divided into three categories: Sacraments of Initiation (Baptism, Confirmation, and Eucharist), Sacraments of Healing (Reconciliation and Anointing the Sick) and Sacraments of Service (Matrimony and Holy Orders)

The celebrations of the sacraments are signs of Jesus' presence in our lives and a means for receiving His grace. As the old Catechism said: "Outward signs of inward grace."

Sacrilege

Sacrilege consists in profaning or treating unworthily the sacraments and other liturgical actions, as well as persons, things, or places consecrated to God. Sacrilege is a grave sin especially when committed against the Eucharist, for in this sacrament the true Body of Christ is made substantially present for us. (2120 - Catechism of the Catholic Church). Latin *sacrilegium*, robbing a temple, from *sacer*, sacred, and *legere*, to purloin.)

Saint

This is someone who, by their life and actions, is an example of holiness. The process by which the

Church declares someone to be a saint can only happen after their death.

There is a four-stage judicial process that each individual case has to go through before being canonised as a saint, which cannot begin until at least five years after their death. It involves taking evidence about the individual's holiness, the scrutiny of their writings and evidence that people are drawn to holiness and prayer through the individual's example.

1. The person is called a "servant of God";

2. The person is called "venerable";
3. That person is beatified and declared "blessed" (requires a miracle attributed to the person's intercession);
4. Finally, the person is canonised as a saint for veneration by the universal Church (requires a further authenticated miracle).

It is important to note that the Faithful venerate saints and do not adore or worship them. Prayers to saints are intercessory prayers, asking them to intercede for the faithful to God. Statues and pictures of saints honour and memorialise them, just as the statue of a famous general or politician honours that person.

Sacristan

A Sacristan is traditionally defined as "An officer who is charged with the care of the sacristy, the church, and their contents". In parish life, this is one of the roles that is rarely seen by parishioners.  It is a "behind-the-scenes" position that makes the priest's job on Sundays less stressful.

The General Instruction of the Roman Missal explains, "The following also exercise(s) a liturgical function: The sacristan, who carefully arranges the liturgical books, the vestments, and other things necessary in the celebration of the Mass".

Today this is regarded as one of the Lay Liturgical Ministries, and it is a crucial one to ensure the smooth running of the Mass and other liturgies.

Sacristy/Vestry

A sacristy is the room in a Catholic church where religious and sacred objects used during the liturgies are stored. Things like the chalices, altar linens, and holy oils are kept in a sacristy.

A vestry is the room where priests change into their vestments. While vestments might might be stored in a vestry, most other holy objects are kept in the sacristy. The word literally means "repository for sacred things," from the Latin root *sacer,* "sacred."

However, due to space constraints and practicality, the sacristy and vestry are usually combined into one room in most modern churches.

Sanctuary

The Holy of Holies - that part of the church where the priest, assisted by servers and other ministers, celebrates the Eucharist, and from which the Word is spo-ken. It is generally set apart by a raised floor or special decoration to show its importance.

Sanctuary Lamp

The sanctuary lamp was tradi-tionally a wax candle housed in a red glass container near the tabernacle in a church or chapel. It is an emblem of Christ's abiding love and a reminder to the faithful to respond with loving adoration in return. The candle is kept burning all the time the Blessed Sacrament is present. Today, however, these lamps are more practically oil or electric lamps.

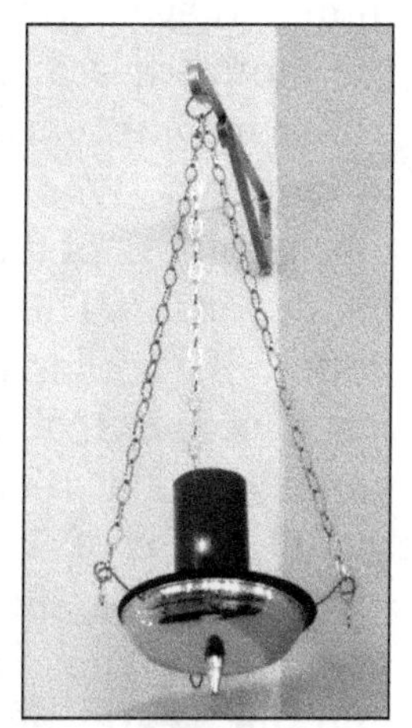

Scapular

There are two types of scapular, the monastic and devotional scapular, although both forms may simply be referred to as "scapulars".

The **monastic scapular** is a somewhat large length of cloth suspended both front and back from the shoulders of the wearer, often reaching to just above the feet. It may vary in shape, colour, size and style. Monastic scapulars originated as aprons worn by medieval monks and were later extended to habits for members of religious organisations, orders or confraternities.

The **<u>devotional scap-
ular</u>** is a much smaller
item and evolved from
the monastic scapular.
These may be worn by
individuals who are
not members of a mo-
nastic order. The de-
votional scapular typ-
ically consists of two
small (usually rectan-

gular) pieces of cloth, wood or laminated paper, a few
centimetres in size, which may bear religious images or texts. These are joined by two bands of fabric,
and the wearer places one square on the chest, rests
the bands one on each shoulder and lets the second
square drop down the back. As an object of popular
piety, the devotional scapular serves to remind the
wearers of their commitment to live a Christian life.

See

An Episcopal See is the area of a bishop's jurisdiction and can be synonymous with "Diocese". The
word See is derived from the Latin *sedes*, which in
its original or proper sense denotes the seat or chair
that, in the case of a bishop, is the earliest symbol of
the bishop's authority. An Archbishop's See can include several dioceses in his Province. The most well-
known See is the Holy See in the Vatican, which is the
Episcopal See of the Pope.

Seminary

A Seminary is a tertiary educational institution or college for educating students ("**Seminarians**") in scripture, theology, and so forth, generally to prepare them for ordination. Picture: St John Vianney Seminary in Pretoria, South Africa.

Small Christian Community

Small Christian Communities (SCCs) are groups of parishioners who meet regularly, usually once a month, in the comfortable setting of one of the members' homes. They are modeled on the early church communities: gatherings of small home-based communities, where sharing of life and faith may occur; a place where members support one another and get to know one another personally.

Sponsor

A Sponsor is a baptised and confirmed person who assists and accompanies recipients of the Sacraments of Initiation - in the Sacrament of Baptism, sponsors are commonly called Godparents.

Stations of the Cross

The Stations of the Cross, or the **Way of the Cross**, also known as the Way of Sorrows or the *Via Crucis*, refers to a series of images depicting Jesus Christ on the day of his crucifixion, which are used in a devotion that follows Jesus on his way to Calvary through prayer and reflection. The stations grew out of imitations of the Via Dolorosa in Jerusalem, which is believed to be the actual path Jesus walked to Calvary. The object of the Stations is to help the Christian faithful to make a spiritual pilgrimage through contemplation of the Passion of Christ. There are fourteen moments in the Lord's Passion that are particularly remembered in the Stations of the Cross. There can also be a fifteenth Station, depicting the Resurrection.

Stipend vs Stole Fees

In the Catholic Church, a Mass stipend is a donation given by the laity to a priest for praying a Mass. Despite the name, which usually means salary or wages, it is considered as a gift or offering (Latin: *stips*) freely given rather than a payment (Latin: *stipendium*) as such. Stole fees include offerings for baptisms, weddings, funerals, house blessings and other associated blessings, such as car blessings. Stole fees are an ancient tradition of the Catholic Church, and there is a provision of Canon Law (848) that the faithful should give an offering for the administration of the sacraments as determined by the competent authority.

Stole

A stole is a strip of cloth about two to three metres long and about 10 cm wide. The priest wears the stole over the alb with the centre around the back of the neck and the two ends hanging in front. The deacon wears the stole over his left shoulder, and it drapes across his body, clasped on the right side.

Stoles are often decorated in some way and are the same colour as the chasuble.

There is also a smaller stole which is usually carried with the priest and is used in the confessional, and also when administering the Anointing of the Sick. It is commonly purple.

Surplice

The surplice is in the form of a tunic of white linen or cotton fabric, reaching to the knees, with wide or moderately full sleeves. The surplice is meant to be a miniature alb, the alb itself being the symbol of the white garment received at Baptism.

It is often worn by seminarians when attending Mass and by non-clerical choirs. It is usually worn over a cassock and never alone, nor is it ever gathered by a belt or cincture. The surplice belongs to the *vestes sacrae* (sacred vestments), though it requires no blessing before it is worn.

Synod vs Council

In the history of the Church, synods were normally held locally, within various regions of the world, to deal with local disciplinary issues. Pope Paul VI revived this idea and established the Synod of Bishops in 1965 with the *Motu Proprio Apostolica Sollicitudo.*

The current Code of Canon Law details the purpose of these smaller groups of bishops who meet together to discuss various topics.

The Synod of Bishops is a group of bishops who have been chosen from different regions of the world and meet together at fixed times to foster closer unity between the pope and the bishops, to assist the pope with their counsel in the preservation and growth of faith and morals and in the observance and strengthening of ecclesiastical discipline, and to consider questions pertaining to the activity of the Church in the world.

According to the Catholic Encyclopedia, "Councils are legally convened assemblies of ecclesiastical dignitaries and theological experts for the purpose of discussing and regulating matters of church doctrine and discipline."

In particular, "Ecumenical Councils are those to which the bishops, and others entitled to vote, are convoked from the whole world (*oikoumene*) under the presidency of the pope or his legates, and the decrees of which, having received papal confirmation, bind all Christians."

Most recently, the Second Vatican Council (Vatican II - 1962–1965 - pictured) was convened to address the many new challenges that the Church had to face in the modern world. This assembly in Rome of bishops of the World convoked by Pope John XXIII and was referred to as an Ecumenical Council. Approximately 2 500 bishops were in attendance at this the most major event in the Church's recent history. It set the Church on the course of renewal.

Synoptic Gospels

Seeing through one lens. Matthew, Mark, and Luke are called "Synoptic Gospels" because they can be "seen together." What that actually means is that these Gospels contain many of the same stories, and that those stories are sometimes even presented in the same sequence within each of the three different synoptic Gospels.

Tabernacle

The tabernacle is a spe-cial box or small cup-board in which the Blessed Sacrament is stored outside of Mass. The Eucharist can be taken from the tabernacle for distribution to the sick or to place in a monstrance for Benediction and Adora-tion. The tabernacle may be located in the sanctuary or in a chapel to the side of the

sanctuary. Normally made of metal - other materials such as wood can also be used - the tabernacle is of-ten decorated with symbols associated with the Eucharist, such as loaves and fish, a lamb or, as in the case of the one in the illustration, the *chi-ro* (Greek symbol for *Christos*). The Church requires that all tabernacles be immovable (fixed) and that they must have a lock.

Thurible

The thurible, also called a censer, is the vessel used in the liturgy for the burning of aromatic incense strewn on lighted coals, for use to incense articles and people as part of certain liturgies and celebrations.

Note: There is a giant thurible weighing about 80 kg at the Cathedral of Santiago de Campostella in Spain, called the *Botafumeiro*. It's now only used for special occasions. The Botafumeiro is suspended from the ceiling by ropes and takes eight men in red robes called *tiraboleiros* (incense carriers) to get it swinging. Once it's moving, it can hit speeds of up to 70 km per hour! See https://youtu.be/2QFd_55El1I.

Thurifer

This is the person (altar server) who carries the thurible. Many Catholics often get the terms confused, calling a thurible a thurifer!

Transept

The transept is that part of a church, particularly in older churches and especially medieval churches, which forms a cross with the nave of the church.

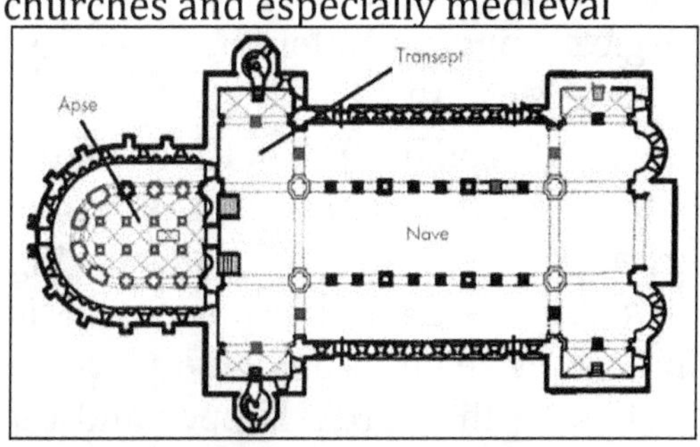

Transubstantiation

Transubstantiation is the conversion of the substance of the Eucharistic elements into the body and blood of Christ at consecration, only the appearances of bread and wine still remaining. The Catholic doctrine of transubstantiation states that the bread and wine, at the moment of consecration during Holy Mass, actually become the Body and Blood of Jesus Christ. The change, however, is not detectable by the senses.

Triduum

Sundown on Holy Thursday to sundown on Easter Sunday is considered the most solemn part of the liturgical year. This three-day period is referred to as the Easter Triduum, also known as the Sacred Triduum, or Paschal Triduum. It is the summit of the Liturgical Year. Though chronologically three days, they are liturgically one day unfolding for us the unity of Christ's Paschal Mystery.

The single celebration of the Triduum marks the end of the Lenten season and leads to the Mass of the Resurrection of the Lord at the Easter Vigil.

First Day — Thursday sunset to Friday sunset. Two important celebrations take place, namely the celebration of the Lord's Supper and the celebration of the Lord's Passion. The presentation of the Sacred Oils, the collection for the poor and the Vigil following the procession to the Altar of Repose in the chapel all form part of the first day of the Triduum.

Second Day — Runs from sunset Friday to sunset on Saturday. This is the day of the Lord's death. In order to keep our minds and hearts focused throughout the day, we need to create times for prayer and recollection. This calls for discipline and refraining from all unnecessary activity so that our minds remain tuned to the mystery unfolding within us and around us.

Third Day — Runs from Saturday sunset to Sunday sunset and is known as the Day of the Lord's Resurrection.

Triregnum

The triregnum is the tiara or crown traditionally worn by popes and last worn at a coronation by Pope St Paul VI *(right)*. It is shaped like a beehive and decorated with precious stones and pearls. The tiara is formed by three crowns that symbolise the three powers of the Pope: father of kings, governor of the world and Vicar of

Christ. Pope Paul VI gave his tiara to the poor, but Popes John Paul II, Benedict and Francis were gifted crowns by various groups or countries. These crowns were never officially worn. On the left is the crown given to Pope Francis by Macedonia.

V

Vatican vs Holy See vs Apostolic See

When one mentions the Holy See, most people think of Vatican City and mistakenly use the terms interchangeably. The confusion is made worse by the fact that the Pope is the head of both Vatican City and the Holy See. However, Vatican City and the Holy See are entirely distinct entities with a different nature, establishment, and functions. The Holy See is the central governing body of the entire Roman Catholic Church located within the Vatican City, an independent State located on the Vatican hill.

Vatican City ("The Vatican") is the smallest country in the world, established by the Lateran Treaty of 1929 between the Kingdom of Italy and the Holy See.

The country is located in Rome and occupies an area of 44 hectares, and houses a population of about 1 000.

The Holy See *(Sancta Sedes)* is an independent sovereign entity and is the top spiritual governing body of the Church. The Bishop of Rome rules through the Roman Curia. The Holy See is the primary diocese and central government of the Roman Catholic Church, with universal authority.

When people say: "The Vatican says...", they are usually actually referring to the Holy See.

An **Apostolic See** is an episcopal See whose foundation is attributed to one or more of the apostles of Jesus or to one of their close associates. The phrase, preceded by the definite article and usually capitalised — "The Apostolic See"— refers to the See of Rome.

Vatican II or Second Vatican Council.

The Second Ecumenical Council of the Vatican, commonly known as the Second Vatican Council, or Vatican II, addressed relations between the Catholic Church and the modern world. The Council, through the Holy See, was formally opened under the pontificate of Pope John XXIII on 11 October 1962 and was closed under Pope Paul VI on the Solemnity of the Immaculate Conception on 8 December 1965. Several changes resulted from the Council, including the renewal of consecrated life with a revised charism, ecumenical efforts towards dialogue with other religions, and the universal call to holiness, which according to Pope Paul VI was "the most characteristic and ultimate purpose of the teachings of the Council".

Veneration of the Cross

The tradition of the Veneration of the Cross dates back to the fourth-century. On Good Friday, the Christians in Jerusalem would gather before a relic of the true cross to kneel, bow, and kiss the cross  in remembrance of the Passion of Christ. Today, most churches venerate the cross during their Good Friday services.

Veneration (of Saints)

Honour, devotion and respect paid to Mary, the Apostles, the martyrs, and to the saints, who, by their intercession and example and in their possession of God, minister to human sanctification, helping the faithful grow in Christian virtue. Venerating the saints does not detract from the glory given to God, since whatever good they possess is a gift from his bounty. Such veneration is often extended to the relics or remains of those recognised as saints; indeed, to many sacred objects and images. Veneration must be clearly distinguished from adoration and worship, which are due to God alone.

Viaticum

The Eucharist received by a dying person. It is the spiritual food for one's "passing over" to the Father from this world. With Penance and the Anointing of the Sick, the reception of Holy Communion as Viaticum constitute the "last sacraments" of the Christian.

Vigil

This is the eve (the evening before) of a religious festival observed by special prayer services and devotional exercises. Traditionally, this has occurred for the major feasts of Easter and Christmas. Vigils can also happen before special occasions, or before funerals, and as special services for a particular intention. The Vigil Mass is now also used to describe the Saturday evening Mass which fulfills the Sunday obligation. The picture shows Catechumens at the Easter Vigil Mass.

Vocation

A calling — all Christians have a vocation to be followers of Christ in the world. Marriage or the single life are also vocations. However, "vocation" is most colloquially used to describe vocations or callings to the priesthood or religious life.

Votive Candle

A votive candle, also called a *prayer candle*, is a small, round candle, sometimes placed in a glass holder. In a church, votive candles are lit for prayer intentions an d are generally placed on a rack or stand.

Some may be placed in front of statues or icons of saints, asking their intercession for the candle lighter's intentions. To "light a candle for someone" indicates one's intention to say a prayer for another person, and the candle symbolises that prayer.

Votive Mass

In the liturgy of the Roman Catholic Church, a Votive Mass (Latin *missa votiva*) is a Mass offered for a *votum*, a special intention. The Mass does not correspond to the Divine Office for the day on which it is celebrated. Examples of Votive Masses are those for all kinds of occasions, including for ordinations, for those about to be baptised, anniversaries of ordinations and professions, for the sick, for marriages, the consecration and dedication of churches and for the dead.

𝖅

𝕽ucchetto

A small skullcap worn by clergy with a knot or braid in the centre. The colour of a zucchetto varies with rank:

• White for the Pope.
• Red for cardinals.
• Purple or violet for bishops.
• Black for the superiors of monasteries (abbots).

Pope Francis' zucchetto has been blown off his head by the wind several times at his outdoor appearances. In September 2014, a zucchetto that formerly belonged to Pope Francis sold for over $110 000 on eBay, with the profits going to charity.

Pronounced *zoo-ket-oh*; Italian *tsook-ket-taw*.

Appendix 1

Sacred Gestures

Dipping the Hand

When you come into the church building, what is the first thing you do? Don't you dip your hand into the holy water and make the sign  of the cross? Why do you do that? Well, for three reasons: a) in repentance for your sins; b) for protection against the Evil One; c) to remind you of your baptism.

Epiclesis

 This is a little known but very important gesture made by the priest just before the consecration. It is known as the Gesture of Epiclesis, and is accompanied by

a prayer invoking the Holy Spirit upon the Eucharistic bread and wine. The gesture entails holding the hands side by side, palms down over the paten and the chalice. It is followed by a blessing (sign of the cross) over the two vessels.

Orans

In the Orans posture, the priest stands with his arms wide. This indicates that he is including everyone present is his prayer. It is interesting to note that, strictly speaking, the congregation should NOT imitate this gesture at any time, especially during the Our Father, but this practice has become widespread, and the Vatican has not specifically come out against it. Even the holding hands at the Our Father is, again strictly speaking, not encouraged.

Preparing for the Gospel

The little book *The Joy of Being Catholic* describes this gesture, as seen through the eyes of an outsider, as "swatting flies". In this gesture, we trace a cross on the forehead, the lips and the heart. In fact, what we are doing is re-affirming our faith and belief in the Word, and preparing ourselves to listen and take it in completely and reverently.

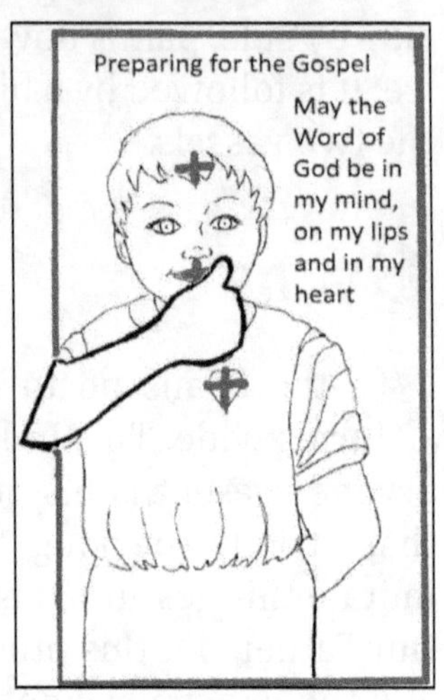

Presentation

The presentation of the Body and Blood of Jesus Christ to the people takes place after the consecration of each specie. Note that it is "after". The consecration occurs when the priest says the words of consecration over the bread and wine – he then presents them to the people by lifting them up, in turn, to signify that they have changed.

The Sign of the Cross

The most common Catholic gesture is the sign of the cross. It symbolically reaffirms two essential Christian doctrines: The Holy Trinity — Father, Son, and Holy Spirit — and humankind's salvation through the cross of Christ. It is interesting to note that the Eastern Catholic Churches make the sign of the cross with the first two fingers joined together, with the thumb touching them at the tip. The three fingers symbolise the Trinity, while the two together symbolise Christ's dual nature - divine and human.

Appendix II

Prayer Postures

The various postures Catholics adopt during Mass are sometimes jokingly referred to as "Catholic Calisthenics", but all have a meaning and a reason.

Bowing & Genuflecting

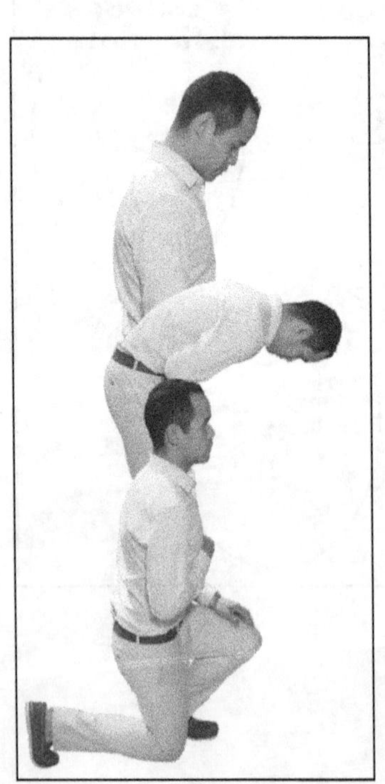

According to the General Instruction of the Roman Missal (GIRM 275), a bow signifies reverence and honour shown to the persons themselves or to the signs that represent them.

There are two kinds of bows: a bow of the head and a bow of the body.

A bow of the head is made when the three Divine Persons are named together and at the names of Jesus, of the Blessed Virgin Mary, and of the Saint in whose honour Mass is being celebrated.

A bow of the body, that is to say, a profound bow, is made to the altar; and at various parts of the liturgy, for example during the Creed at the words *Et incarnatus est* (by the power of the Holy Spirit . . . and became man).

The same kind of bow is made by the deacon when he asks for a blessing before the proclamation of the Gospel. In addition, the priest bows slightly as he speaks the words of the Lord at the consecration.

A genuflection is made by bending the right knee to the ground. It signifies adoration and is reserved for the Most Blessed Sacrament, as well as for the Holy Cross from the solemn adoration during the liturgical celebration on Good Friday until the beginning of the Easter Vigil. The custom of bowing or genuflecting, especially as we enter or leave the church is an expression of our acknowledgement of the presence of Christ.

As one theologian put it: "When we genuflect or bow we are literally saying, 'I believe' without uttering a word. How awesome is that?"

Sitting

The prayer posture of sitting is one of learning, listening and meditation. For example, we sit during the first and second readings (but not for the Gospel because the Gospel has the Words of Jesus, so we stand to respect our Lord). We also sit during the homily (sermon) so that we can listen and learn from the priest as he expands upon the readings and the Gospel.

Standing

The prayer posture of standing is, by far, one of the oldest and most traditional prayer postures. Standing is a posture used to show reverence and respect to Jesus and His Word.

Standing is also the posture we as Catholics use when we pray together. When the priest says "Let us pray", that is generally the cue to stand together in prayer. Standing is also a symbolic reference to the resurrection of Christ.

Kneeling

Kneeling as a prayer posture is also one of prayer and reverence, just like standing. However, kneeling is also a position of supplication and humility.

In the early Church, kneeling signified penance. In the Middle Ages, kneeling came to mean homage, and more recently this posture has come to signify adoration, especially before the presence of Christ in the Eucharist. During Mass, we generally kneel during the Consecration. Kneeling before God is a powerful image of obedience and submission.

Instruction Manual for Mass

When to stand, sit and kneel* CatholicLink

KEY

STAND

SIT

KNEEL

1 FROM THE ENTRANCE PROCESSION UNTIL AFTER THE OPENING PRAYER

2 FIRST READING, PSALM, AND SECOND READING

3 THE ALLELUIA AND THE GOSPEL

4 THE HOMILY

5 THE CREED AND THE PRAYER OF THE FAITHFUL

6 THE OFFERTORY

7 THE PRIEST SAYS "PRAY, BRETHREN..." UNTIL AFTER THE "HOLY, HOLY, HOLY"

8 THE EUCHARISTIC PRAYER UNTIL AFTER THE "AMEN"

9 FROM THE "AMEN" TO AFTER THE "LAMB OF GOD"

10 AFTER THE "LAMB OF GOD"

11 YOU MAY SIT, STAND, OR KNEEL AFTER COMMUNION

12 THE PRAYER AFTER COMMUNION UNTIL THE END OF MASS

*These may vary in some countries and/or dioceses.

143

Appendix III

Catholic Symbols

The Catholic Church uses many different signs and symbols to illustrate various facets of our Faith. Most of these symbols have their roots in the earliest era of the Church, and the use of symbols was especially prevalent during the times of Christian persecution, primarily as a way of identifying oneself as belonging to Christ, to other Christians. They were, if you like, passwords to a community of Christians who themselves were suffering severe persecution.

Christian symbols can be seen carved upon the graves and walls of the early Christian catacombs in Rome.

Symbols can point a way through the spiritual world and act as badges of faith, teaching tools, and aids on the journey towards understanding complex philosophies.

Here are 12 of the most important symbols of Catholicism, along with their very brief descriptions. The list is not by any manner of means complete - these are the ones we would most commonly see and experience.

Let us explore these symbols together.

1. Crucifix

The crucifix is a cross with the figure of the body of Jesus Christ attached to it. This is a distinct Catholic symbol that should be displayed everywhere the Eucharist is celebrated, and often appears in the homes of the faithful. A crucifix is a symbol of sacrifice.

2. Cross

The cross is perhaps the best-known and most universal of all Christian symbols, originating with the crucifixion of our Redeemer. It is revered as a symbol of the victory Christ won through his suffering. As a sign, it recalls Christ Himself and our faith as Christians.

3. Chi-Ro monogram

This is a Greek abbreviation of the title, "Christ". "Chi" and "Rho" are the first two letters in the Greek word Christos or "Christ", although the two letters look like P and X in the English alphabet. Also known as a Christogram.

4. Alpha and Omega

The first and last letters of the Greek alphabet, signifying the Beginning and the End. In the Book of Revelation, Jesus calls Himself the Alpha and the Omega, "The first and the last, the beginning and the end, the one who was, who is, and who is to come." These letters are inscribed on Easter candles.

5. Crossed Keys

A pair of keys that overlap and interlock, creating an "X." This symbol represents the metaphorical keys that Jesus Christ promised to St Peter, empowering him to lead the Church. It symbolises Papal authority.

6. Fish

A sign of the Christian faith for the early Christians during the persecution era. The Greek word for fish is "ICHTHUS"; used by the Christians as an acronym to point to Jesus Christ: **I**esous JESUS; **C**hristos CHRIST; **TH**eou OF GOD; **U**ios SON; **S**oter SAVIOUR.

7. IHS

This is a Christogram for the name of Jesus using the first three letters of the word in Greek. The Greek Christogram **IHΣ**ΟΥΣ (**IHS**OUS) for Jesus, and in Latin **I**esus **H**ominum **S**alvator: "Jesus Saviour of mankind."

8. Dove

The dove is the symbol of the Holy Spirit. When Christ was baptised by John the Baptist, a dove descended on him, according Matthew 3.16 and Mark 1.10. The dove is sometimes depicted with an olive branch in its mouth as a symbol of peace.

9. The Sacred Heart

The heart is a symbol of love, but the Sacred Heart, pierced and wrapped in thorns, shows the depth of Jesus' love. The wound, thorns, and blood represent Jesus' crucifixion, and the flames represent the transformative power of divine love.

10. The Lamb

Christ, the Lamb of God (In Latin: "Agnus Dei"). The whiteness of the Lamb signifies innocence and purity., and is associated with sacrifice. Christ, a sacrificial Lamb, died for our sins. The lamb is sometimes portrayed with a flag and/or a cross, symbolic of Christ's victory over death in his resurrection.

11. Marian Cross

The Marian Cross, as depicted on the Miraculous Medal, describes the symbolic representation of the close connection of Mary with the redemptive mission of Jesus. The letter "M" below the cross indicates Mary's presence at the foot of the cross.

12. Triquetra - Holy Trinity

The Triquetra comes from the Latin noun "trinitas" - "three in one". This symbolises the three persons of the Father, the Son and the Holy Spirit, representing one God. The three equal arcs of the Triquetra stand for equality - the Father, the Son and the Holy Spirit – are all equal, functioning together as one.

Sources

In addition to the dozens of websites and sources that were consulted for the compilation of this book, a proportion of the content is derived from personal knowledge acquired many years in the service of the Church.

Primary among the sources consulted was, perhaps surprisingly, Wikipedia, usually backed up and confirmed by other sources.

Among the other websites consulted were: Vatican.va (the official website of the Holy See), New Advent Catholic Encyclopaedia, Aleteia, Catholic Culture, Catholic Answers, Catholic Words, Catholic Exchange, National Catholic Register, the website of the USCCB (United States Conference of Catholic Bishops), and the Southern Cross (South Africa's Catholic newspaper). One of my primary sources was the website "Dictionary of Catholic Terms" (http://www.thesacredheart.com/dictnary.htm#N)

Secular sources, apart from Wikipedia, include Askdifference.com and Quora.com, as well as dictionaries such as Collins, Webster and Brittanica.

Photographs and Illustrations are for the most part presumed to be in the public domain. Should this not be the case with any particular picture or graphic, kindly contact the publisher using the contact details at the front of the book so that the issue may be rectified.

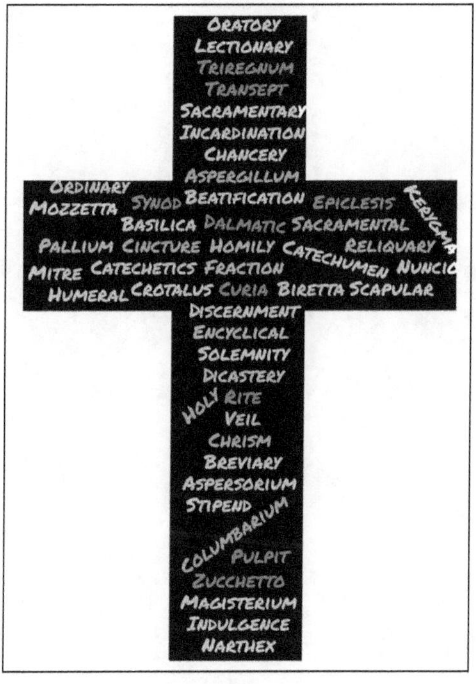

ORATORY
LECTIONARY
TRIREGNUM
TRANSEPT
SACRAMENTARY
INCARDINATION
CHANCERY
ASPERGILLUM

ORDINARY
MOZZETTA SYNOD BEATIFICATION EPICLESIS KERYGMA
BASILICA DALMATIC SACRAMENTAL
PALLIUM CINCTURE HOMILY CATECHUMEN RELIQUARY
MITRE CATECHETICS FRACTION NUNCIO
HUMERAL CROTALUS CURIA BIRETTA SCAPULAR

DISCERNMENT
ENCYCLICAL
SOLEMNITY
DICASTERY
HOLY RITE
VEIL
CHRISM
BREVIARY
ASPERSORIUM
STIPEND
COLUMBARIUM
PULPIT
ZUCCHETTO
MAGISTERIUM
INDULGENCE
NARTHEX